The Dangers of Bus Re-regulation

and Other Perspectives on Markets in Transport

The Dangers of Bus Re-regulation

and Other Perspectives on Markets in Transport

JOHN HIBBS

WITH CONTRIBUTIONS FROM

EAMONN BUTLER

GRAHAM PARKHURST

OLIVER KNIPPING

PAUL KEVILL

The Institute of Economic Affairs

First published in Great Britain in 2005 by
The Institute of Economic Affairs
2 Lord North Street
Westminster
London SW1P 3LB
in association with Profile Books Ltd

The mission of the Institute of Economic Affairs is to improve public understanding of the fundamental institutions of a free society, with particular reference to the role of markets in solving economic and social problems.

A CIP catalogue record for this book is available from the British Library.

ISBN 0 255 36572 1

Typeset in Stone by MacGuru Ltd
info@macguru.org.uk
Printed and bound in Great Britain by Hobbs the Printers

CONTENTS

THE AUTHOR

John Hibbs started work in the bus industry, and when he went to the LSE in 1952 as a research student, his supervisor, the late G. J. Ponsonby, asked him to examine 'the economic consequences of the Road Traffic Act 1930'. The outcome was a thesis in 1954, recommending deregulation. He returned to work in the transport industry, involved first with buses and then British Rail, where he was market research officer for the Eastern Region. Since 1969 he has been in the academic world, but still sees himself more as a busman. He was awarded his doctorate from Birmingham in 1983 for 'a comparative study of bus regulation worldwide'. He is Emeritus Professor of Transport Management at the University of Central England.

FOREWORD

Bus policy receives rather less attention from politicians and economists than rail policy, yet, in most parts of the country, bus travel is far more important. It would be nice to think that the fact that politicians give less attention to bus policy would mean that the industry could be left to its own devices to satisfy consumer demand. Sadly, this is not the case. For decades, until 1985, there was detailed state and municipal control of an industry which was designed to meet the needs of politicians, bureaucrats and trade unions rather than the needs of travellers.

In 1985, radical reform took place that finally allowed bus companies freedom of action to run buses for consumers rather than for politicians. Despite the evident improvements in the industry, since 1997, the Labour government, supported by many local authorities governed by all the major political parties, legislated to provide mechanisms to make the industry accountable to politicians rather than customers once again. The result was 'quality partnerships' and 'quality contracts'. The new legislation is supported by European Union legislation, though it is difficult to see, if the principle of subsidiarity means anything, why the European Union should have anything to do with the mechanisms for regulating buses in Cheltenham, Penzance and Inverness.

Hibbs's analysis and history detailed in the first part of this monograph should be of great interest to anybody involved in policy-making or who is a student or teacher of transport economics. His policy prescription is very short. The 1985 act was well conceived. Nothing has changed to undermine that view and nothing is likely to change. Quality contracts should be repealed and we should return to the status quo that prevailed before the Transport Act 2000. In addition, the development of a proper system of road pricing would allow buses and cars to compete on a level playing field and would enable us to have less regulation of the use of road space to create bus lanes and the like. Hibbs argues that the use of systems of franchise, popular among politicians particularly in the European Union, creates a 'competition for a monopoly' and does not serve the consumer interest.

John Hibbs played a leading role in the academic analysis that was a necessary antecedent of the 1985 Transport Act. This monograph is partly a celebration of John Hibbs's career and of his contribution to the widespread acceptance of the principles of the 1985 act. The monograph will be published on the twentieth anniversary of the act. It also provides a warning to those policy-makers, politicians and academics who believe that markets should be accountable to people rather than to politicians and bureaucrats that, when a landmark act such as the 1985 Transport Act is passed, it is not the end of the battle.

The IEA is pleased that four eminent commentators have added their analysis to that of John Hibbs, in Part 2 of Occasional Paper 137. The chapters by Eamonn Butler, Graham Parkhurst, Oliver Knipping and Paul Kevill are partly intended as a tribute to John Hibbs, but they also analyse specific policy issues that face the transport industry today and which need to be addressed by policy-makers. Taking these contributions as a whole, the message is clear. Markets have done a great deal of good in the bus industry where they have been allowed to operate. Markets are still absent in crucial respects, however – particularly with regard to the pricing and allocation of road space.

As in all IEA publications, the views expressed in Occasional Paper 137 are those of the authors, not those of the Institute (which has no corporate view), its managing trustees, Academic Advisory Council members or senior staff.

PHILIP BOOTH
Editorial and Programme Director,
Institute of Economic Affairs
Professor of Insurance and Risk Management,
Sir John Cass Business School, City University
October 2005

SUMMARY

- The philosophy that underpinned government intervention in the bus industry was first formally outlined in 1919 by Sir Eric Geddes. This philosophy was progressively implemented during the 1920s and 1930s.
- From 1930 bus operators required a service licence. This remained in place for 55 years, and the adverse consequences of this constraint on market entry and competition are still with us.
- As the government intervened more, cartels were reinforced and economic rationality in pricing and management was jettisoned. The railways were favoured by policy-makers and the growing potential for transport by road was not properly understood. Coordination of services by central direction replaced coordination using the price mechanism.
- From 1947 to the late 1960s the bus industry was gradually taken into state ownership. A steep decline ensued, encouraged by the use of 'average cost pricing'. Routes that did not cover average costs but which nevertheless covered marginal costs and made a contribution to overheads tended to be over-priced and would often be shut down.
- From the late 1960s onwards, local authorities used their powers to subsidise the bus industry. Having lost the

principle of marginal cost pricing, the bus industry then lost any incentive to control costs at all.

- The 1979 Conservative government liberalised some aspects of long-distance coach travel and freight haulage. This was accompanied by limited privatisation.
- The 1985 Transport Act led to the privatisation of the National Bus Company, the gradual privatisation of municipal bus operations and the replacement of licensing with the registration of bus services.
- Theoretically, the replacement of licensing with registration removed the impediments to competition and innovation. Many benefits flowed from this, but the market was slow to react. Over time, the bus industry responded to the new environment, in many places showing considerable growth.
- The latest government intervention, the Transport Act 2000, is a monumental intrusion into the freedom of transport management in Britain. Quality contracts reopen the possibilities for substantial regulation and control by local authorities. Franchise, or 'competition for a monopoly', is a likely outcome. The new situation makes it likely that many local authorities will put the needs of buses second to the needs of grandiose, expensive and impractical tramway schemes.
- UK government regulation is reinforced by regulation from the European Union. The clock has been turned back and we need to return to the principles of the 1985 Transport Act. A welcome development, though, is the fact that road pricing is firmly on the political agenda. If road space is not properly priced, buses face a competitive disadvantage and, furthermore, local politicians feel a need to intervene in the allocation of scarce road space.

TABLES, FIGURES AND BOXES

The Dangers of Bus Re-regulation

and Other Perspectives on Markets in Transport

PART 1: THE DANGERS OF BUS RE-REGULATION

1 THE STORY OF GOVERNMENT MEDDLING, PART ONE

The politics of intervention

Transport is an activity of such central importance for the needs of people in society and for the health of the economy that it is surprising to see how weak is its status and how little it is understood. Yet the extent to which it is by nature fail-dangerous has invited state interference ever since the mechanisation of the railways. This means that any discussion of the function and ownership of the bus industry must respect the differences between safety regulation (so-called quality control) and direct or indirect interference with the freedom of managers to succeed in running the business. Quantity control, which limits freedom of entry and exit, confers an element of monopoly upon the firms within its limits, while price control removes the firm from the benefits of the market, with serious consequences for the economy.

Throughout the 'railway age' there was concern lest the companies should exploit their supposed monopoly power, which led in 1921 to the close regulation of rates and fares (the concern has been shown to have been largely misplaced in view of the growing volume of freight moved by road throughout the period; see Barker and Gerhold, 1993). Between 1919 and 1939 road motor transport subjected the railway companies to increasing competition, and the 'solution' of total state ownership of the railways, attempted in 1947, was quickly found to be mistaken. The movement of goods takes place today in a market situation, subject to safety control, whether by road, rail, coastwise shipping or pipeline. By contrast, passenger movement has never obtained the same freedom, apart from the use of the motor car, which dominates the sector, and more recently by the expansion of internal air services at low cost.

While buses were horse-drawn there was little intervention in the business. In some cities there would appear to have been a cartel to protect the interests of existing firms, but the market was always open to newcomers and exit was easy. In the metropolis the cartel came to be dominated after 1856 by the London General Omnibus Company (LGOC), but new entrants continued to develop the trade, becoming accepted when they survived direct competition. The omnibus seems to have been popular with all classes; there is a picture of Mr Gladstone riding in one. The horses made streets dirty, and occasionally dangerous when one bolted with the remains of a cart behind it, so the use of cabs and buses made travel easier and more pleasant. The new form of transport, copied in other cities, offered improved access which previously had been limited to those who could afford a carriage or to hire a cab, and it expanded choice for those who otherwise could only walk. The process that began in London with Shillibeer's omnibus in 1829 was to continue until the motor car radically altered the pattern of demand.

The efficiency of the omnibus was limited by the state of the highway, and the growth of railways demonstrated the mechanical advantage of steel wheels on steel rails. This was first applied to street transport in New York in 1832 and it was copied in Paris in 1853.

Early schemes based on steel tracks in Britain were unwelcome, and several attempts failed, but the technology was improved, and following the success of a line opened in Liverpool in 1869 horse-drawn tramcars were increasingly used in British cities. It was at this point that intervention started to appear, contributing in due course to the dominance of the municipal tramway, a mode of transport fashionable today in the form of Light Rapid Transit.

The construction of street tramways required authority for the disturbance of the highway, and for this purpose the first companies obtained parliamentary powers. The Tramways Act of 1870 (see Yelton, 2004) simplified the procedure, but at the same time it gave local authorities considerable powers of both veto and compulsory purchase, which did not apply to omnibuses. Tramway companies were made responsible for the repair and maintenance of the highway between the tracks and for 18 inches on each side of them, and they were required to replace the highway if the line was abandoned. In addition to this financial burden most orders and acts imposed low maximum fares, and so there began the practice of interference with managerial freedom that was later to undermine the efficiency of the motor bus industry.

The 1870 act enabled local authorities to construct tramways, but they could be operated only by lessees. Many councils in due course obtained their own operating powers, and with the application of mechanical traction, at first by steam or cable and then by electricity, the industry at the start of the twentieth century was predominantly in municipal ownership and control. The first 'motor omnibus' service commenced in Edinburgh in 1898, two years after the Locomotives on Highways Act had emancipated the motor car, while Eastbourne council obtained powers in 1902 to operate motor buses, to be followed by many other authorities, most of them already owning their tramways. In London the last horse bus service ended in 1914 and the last horse-drawn trams went a year later. By then the motor bus was established in London and increasingly in most other parts of the country.

After 1918 public road passenger transport grew rapidly in both rural and urban contexts. Some railway companies had started running motor buses sooner, notably the Great Western, which had done so without any statutory power. Alongside a growing number of small firms, the larger businesses developed a form of cartel, each of them seeking a territorial monopoly. Long-distance coach services appeared in 1925 and by 1930 they covered the whole of England, while coach tours, at home and on the Continent, began to appear shortly after 1918. Much neglected both then and now, small firms spread to develop what may be called 'the coaching trade', offering better-quality vehicles for private hire and also using them for local services, especially in rural areas.

The state moves in

In London various conflicts of interest between the underground railways and the buses led to a settlement in 1912 whereby the LGOC, then a motor bus operator, was sold to the London Electric Railway, a company headed by Alfred Stanley, who later, as Lord Ashfield, was to play an important part in the ending of competition (a consequence of this was that the major bus interests were left to develop the cartel in the provinces). Short-sighted management decisions led to a shortage of buses in the post-World War I years, and on 5 August 1922 new competition appeared in the form of the 'Chocolate Express', so named after the vehicles' livery. Its success attracted 500 'pirate' buses on to the streets within eighteen months, and they competed with the municipal and company tramways as well as with the LGOC buses, which as a result began to operate over the tramway routes which had formerly been protected. The new competition was financially disastrous for the combine, and not least for the tramways, given that the London County Council (LCC) system was by then being subsidised from the rates. When the LCC announced a cut in tramwaymen's wages in 1924 the outcome was a strike, joined by the LGOC busmen, organised by Ernest Bevin's new Transport and General Workers' Union. Only the 'pirates' continued running.

Ashfield, along with Sir Eric Geddes, had been working for some time to consolidate the ownership of public transport in London. Geddes had even broader objectives. When he introduced a bill in 1919 to set up a Ministry of Transport he told the Commons that it was nothing short of criminal to continue the system of competition between trams and road services. In those days parliamentary approval was required to set up a new ministry, and his original proposal for a ministry to control 'railways, light railways, tramways, canals and inland navigations, roads, bridges, vehicles and traffic and the supply of electricity', with powers of nationalisation, was drastically cut down before it could be enacted. Geddes became the first minister, but what may be called 'the Geddes philosophy' remains, still present in policy proposals today. In his presidential address at the inaugural meeting of the Institute of Transport in 1920, he spoke of a bargain that had to be struck between the community and the transport providers with the former granting to the latter monopoly status in return for efficient and economic services, with charges controlled to prevent abuse of the monopoly while ensuring the enterprise an adequate rate of return on investment.[1] Like Ashfield, Geddes was commited to what he saw as the unity of transport.

While the new ministry was to be preoccupied by railway policy, it soon looked at the fast-growing bus industry, and a departmental committee was set up. But Bevin's threat to call out the Tube drivers in support of the busmen and tramwaymen meant that intervention could not be delayed, and a bill was rushed through Parliament to become the London Traffic Act 1924. Bus competition was forbidden, and the London operators found themselves with monopoly rights in their services, which led most of the smaller ones to sell their businesses to the LGOC. This then led to the formation in 1933 of the London Passenger Transport Board, which may be seen as a forerunner of public ownership of the industry, though it fell short of the full state ownership that Herbert Morrison had desired.

The London and Home Counties Traffic Advisory Committee, set up under the 1924 act, and the Departmental Committee on the Licensing and Regulation of Public Service Vehicles contributed between them to much of what was to become the Road Traffic Act 1930, the consequences of which for the bus industry are to be felt up to the present day. As Chester (1936) was to conclude, the principles that it adduced were 'priority, protection, and public need'. The essential distinction between 'quality' and 'quantity' control, with which this paper commences, was never recognised, while from the start there seems to have been an assumption that price control should be introduced.

1 I am indebted to Kevin Hey for drawing my attention to Geddes's speech, which appears to have been well received by a distinguished institute, which sadly has ceased to exist.

Neither were these issues debated by the Royal Commission on Transport of 1929–31, which was set up with the objective of increased coordination (see Box 1).

Box 1 The terms of reference for the Royal Commission on Transport, 1929–31

The terms of reference were '... to take into consideration the problems arising out of the growth of road traffic and, with a view to securing the employment of the available means of transport in Great Britain (including transport by sea coast-wise and by ferries) to the greatest public advantage, to consider and report what measures, if any, should be adopted for their better regulation and control, and, so far as is desirable in the public interest, to promote their coordinated working and development'.

The commission had before it a draft licensing system prepared by the departmental committee and submitted by the ministry. After hearing evidence from local government and from the cartel (but none from the independent bus operators) it recommended this system, with certain modifications, in its Second Report in 1929. Many witnesses had dwelt on the supposed problems of competition, such as 'skimming the cream of the traffic', and on the need for subsidising 'unremunerative services'; arguments that Ponsonby (Ponsonby, 1958) was later to demolish. In a memorable interchange, one of the members of the commission accused R. J. Howley of British Electric Traction (a cartel representative) of 'going dangerously near telling us a monopoly is less efficient than those with whom you are competing'.[2]

Before 1931 the licensing of omnibuses and their services had been governed by the Town Police Clauses Acts of 1847 and 1889 and the Stage Carriage Act of 1832. These might or might not be adopted by local authorities and, in any case, could be adopted only by urban authorities. Also, they were largely unsuitable for the motorised industry, though they were loosely enough defined to permit its rapid growth after 1919. They were replaced by the system of licensing introduced under the Road Traffic Act 1930, which closely reflected the Second Report of the Royal Commission, with one important change: instead of being administered by local government, the act set up area traffic commissioners, free of political interference.

The principles of Geddes and Ashfield and the idea of franchise had already appeared in the debates over public transport that were to lead to the 1930 act. The advisory committee had been invited to consider the system of 'concessions' already to be found on the Continent. But while these were not introduced, the management of bus and coach businesses came to lose much of its freedom. Route monopolies were set up, as they had been in London in 1924, so that ownership was consolidated, but two constraints lay at the heart of the new system which were to distort both economic efficiency and customer satisfaction for a period of 50 years, and which continue to exist in the proposals for franchise which we have before us today. From 1931, outwith much of the coaching trade, any innovation was virtually certain to be met with an objection, from another operator or from the

2 Minutes of Evidence, Question 5589.

railway companies, which inhibited any attempt by management to respond to changes in settlement and demand. The 'territorial operators' – the cartels – were entrenched, while local authority transport continued to function in a world detached from market forces. Alongside this the new regulators, the area traffic commissioners, imposed, increasingly after 1950, a method of price control based on average costing over large areas which removed from management the very heart of commercial freedom: freedom to set the price of the product. The Geddes philosophy can be seen in all this, but it must not be forgotten that the representatives of the cartel had made little protest before the Royal Commission, at which the multitude of small firms was not represented.

The new act required all bus operators to hold four types of quality licence, designed to ensure safety of both vehicles and staff. While they were a barrier to entry there was justification for them in a fail-dangerous industry like transport. It was the road service licence which introduced quantity regulation and price control, and it was to be this which was no longer required after 1985. Nevertheless, its impact is to be felt even now, and the consequences are with us still. Any application for a new service or improvement to an existing one was likely to meet objection from existing operators as well as from the railway companies, so that reaction to market demand became expensive and difficult to achieve.

The consequences of regulation

The immediate impact of the 1930 act was to encourage consolidation of ownership. The problems of the Depression combined with the ageing of vehicles bought ten years earlier led many small firms to sell out, at prices that could never have been obtained in an open market.[3] But it was the changes to the cartel that were to have the greater and longer-lasting significance, as the big players adapted to the new situation.

That the new legislation would follow the Geddes convictions could have been foreseen without waiting for the Royal Commission to report, for, as we have seen, the bill that it recommended had been drafted by the departmental committee. Despite strong opposition, the four mainline railway companies obtained powers in August 1928 to operate road services (the Great Western legalising its operations at this late date). Later in the same year they met with representatives of the cartel, with a view to the railways investing in the member companies, but without taking a controlling interest. There followed a tense period of negotiations, at the end of which the cartel had extended its membership, and the railways had agreed to take no more than a 49 per cent shareholding in any of the companies.[4] One consequence was to be the investment of some £6 million by the railways, enabling the further acquisition of competing operators by the territorial companies.

While the railway settlement of 1929 repeated the London settlement of 1924 and looked to the attempts at coordination of 1947, the long-lasting consequence of the new system was to be the control of prices by the traffic commissioners. The road service licence severely inhibited change and innovation, but it is an open

3 The cartel was based on 'area agreements' which ensured that member companies would not normally compete across their borders. A consequence was that smaller firms operating in such places often found it hard to find a purchaser, and to this day they tend to exist along the same borders.

4 On this see Hibbs (1989: 98–107). The railways also entered into agreements at this time with certain municipal authorities running bus and tramway services.

question as to how far the traffic commissioners had authority to impose fare tables on every road service licence, which they did, usually at the prices previously being charged. The act stated that 'The Commissioners shall satisfy themselves that the fares charged or proposed to be charged are reasonable and, if representations are made to them and if they consider it in the public interest, may, after holding a public enquiry, fix maximum and minimum fares for any service in their Area'. Little use of these powers appears to have been made until increases in fuel tax in the budgets of 1951 and 1952 forced operators to apply to increase their fares.

The railway companies objected to a large number of initial applications, but the commissioners generally applied the principle of 'grandfather rights', with one major exception. Railway objections to licences for express coach services stressed the impact of their competition, since their fares were generally much lower than those for equivalent journeys by train, reflecting the cross-subsidy required to maintain branch line and stopping services.[5] Whether by coincidence or design, the commissioners generally responded by imposing a limit on the number of vehicles permitted on each journey, and while the impact of this was limited by the reduction in travel during the Depression, it was to be felt more strongly in the period of increased demand of the post-war years.

Summary – freedom or franchise?

The industry was now sheltered from internal competition, and

5 The average cost per passenger-mile was in fact lower for express trains than for coach services.

while the quality regulations were justified in principle, quantity and price control were to become major problems when, in later years, the car became a significant mode of transport. The pattern of thought was not limited to passenger transport. The Royal Commission had expressed concern about the organisation of the road freight business, which it said was given to 'bitter and uneconomic strife' (i.e. competition). It called for licensing in order to 'organise' the industry so as to improve 'co-ordination'. There followed the Salter Conference of 1932, at which the multitude of small hauliers had no representation, and in due course the Road and Rail Traffic Act 1933 introduced tight quantity control, save for own-account operators, but minimum safety regulation. Here again the railway companies were given the right to object to any application for change to a licence.

The freedom for commercial management of the bus and coach industry had been progressively constrained ever since Sir Eric Geddes presented Parliament with his planned 'Ministry of Ways and Communications' in 1919. Transport policy throughout the period failed to recognise that the growth of road transport had put an end to the threat of railway monopoly dating from the late nineteenth century. In their different ways Lord Ashfield, Ernest Bevin and Herbert Morrison worked for the establishment of a cross-modal monopoly for London's passenger transport, and while this was a harbinger for nationalisation in 1947 their thinking contributed to the work of the Royal Commission, and the Road Traffic Act 1930, as far as provincial bus services were concerned.

The contestability of the industry was now severely limited, while the central freedom of management, to control prices, was proscribed. The term franchise had appeared in the literature, and the idea was implicit in the attitude of some of the tramway-owning local authorities as early as the 1920s.[6] What is remarkable is the extent to which the larger 'territorial' companies, the cartel, accepted the way policy was going, while the smaller firms were given no say. *Coordination* was the watchword of the period, though just what it should mean in practice was seldom defined.

6 Some councils used their powers under the Town Police Clauses Acts with the idea of franchise very much in mind.

2 THE STORY OF GOVERNMENT MEDDLING, PART TWO

The state takes over

The Labour government elected in 1945 moved quickly to expropriate the private ownership of the public transport industry. The philosophy once again was patently that of Geddes, but the structure of the new British Transport Commission (BTC) was something of a compromise. The various executives had considerable independence and the powers of the commission were weakened from the start since the members of the executives were appointed by the Minister of Transport and not by the BTC. Each then pursued its own agenda to the extent that the Road Haulage Executive systematically poached traffic from the railways, while the Railway Executive committed itself to the retention and development of steam traction, plainly contrary to the policy of the commission.

A problem arose here from a behavioural constraint not recognised by Geddes or Ashfield, which is the personal commitment, at all levels, to the particular mode of transport within which people choose to work. Even within the Railway Executive there were quite radical differences between those working for one or another of the regions, harking back to company days, and these remained until the business was split on a functional basis in the 1970s. There are radical differences between rail and road transport management, between passenger and freight, and between land, sea and air, and these must be important for the efficient provision of services. Quite apart from the problems of scale that must undermine any attempt to form a single transport monopoly, there is the loyalty of people to their chosen mode, which must mean that any attempt to identify a 'transportant' is bound to fail.

The Transport Act of 1947 immediately nationalised the four railway companies and converted the London Passenger Transport Board into a state-owned executive, which continued to function much as it had done before. The commission was given the duty of acquiring the road haulage industry, except for firms operating within a 25-mile radius of their base, and traders carrying their own goods, which remained under the 1933 licensing system. Part IV of the act, headed 'Other Forms of Transport', suggests that the bus industry was not seen as a priority, 'Passenger Road Services' being dealt with in three sections. The act gave the BTC powers to 'secure the provision' of such services, but Part IV merely allowed the design of 'area schemes' for submission to the ministry, which would include the acquisition of operators within such areas and the organisation of suitable bodies to run the services. Doubtless this was seen to be a step towards the Geddes vision of 'the unity of transport', but the BTC was never in effective overall control. In 1948 Gilbert Walker described the outcome of the act as 'one of the least promising forms of business organisation yet devised by man' (see Savage, 1985: 183).

Work started on a Passenger Road Transport Scheme for the north-eastern area, which appeared in August 1949. It provided for the acquisition of 214 businesses, eight of which were municipal operators, and the Labour-controlled councils in the area vigorously resisted the loss of their buses and trams. By then Sir Frederick Heaton, chairman of the Tilling group of bus companies, had announced the sale of its subsidiaries to the commission, which then proceeded to acquire the Scottish Motor Traction group and the Red & White companies in South Wales and southern England. Other purchases followed, and in June 1949 a new Road Passenger Executive was set up by the commission to be responsible for them all, and to pursue the area schemes. It was generally expected that the sale of the British Electric Traction (BET) group would follow, but the board was against it, and the chairman, H. C. Drayton, announced that he would fight nationalisation 'to the last wheel'.

The 1947 act exempted the commission from the licensing requirements of the Road Traffic Act 1930, but an early decision was made to ignore this, and the state-owned bus companies continued to work under the 1930 licensing system, except for London Transport, which was exempt within its 'special area'. Two challenges to this were overridden in the courts (see Yelton, 2004: 80), stretching the letter of the law to the satisfaction of the BTC. One very important consequence, which is still resonant today, was to retain the control of fares at the stage when the traffic commissioners were starting to apply standard charging to all services over wide areas of the country. The comparison of average cost with average revenue per mile became standard practice, and price discrimination was ruled out.

In 1951, and again in 1952, the problems of the balance of payments led to a sharp increase in fuel tax in each year. The bus operators, whose prices were now closely regulated, were obliged to apply to the area traffic commissioners for an increase, the territorial companies taking the initiative. While it is not clear how far the chairmen of commissioners coordinated their response, the outcome was to impose a standard rate per passenger-mile on the services of each company over the whole of its area, the actual rate varying from one business to another. Smaller operators were not always required to use the same rate, but standard prices were generally imposed on them also.

Price discrimination intended to respond to demand was now forbidden, with serious consequences (see Box 2 for an example).

Box 2 The consequences of rigid costing and pricing

A small business that had been set up after World War I in northern Hertfordshire ran a daily service between two market towns, Royston and Bishop's Stortford. Of the two, Bishop's Stortford was the greater attraction, so the fares in that direction were set at a lower rate. So as to serve as many settlements as possible on each journey, there were various diversions, including a 'double run' of several miles. When a standard rate was enforced the relative price advantage was lost while many fares were sharply increased to reflect the actual mileage involved. As a result fewer journeys were made (not least because car ownership was growing) and it was said that in school holidays the oldest child under fourteen, still eligible for a child's fare, would be sent to do the family shopping.

The policy is reminiscent of the fixing of railway rates under the Railway Act 1921, and the outcome was inevitably the same shift away from management and towards administration, so that for the next 30 years (and more) the focus was to be on running buses, not carrying passengers 'for hire and reward'. The standard rates were calculated from the average cost per vehicle-mile submitted by the territorial company, which would then be seen as a benchmark against which to set the average revenue for each service, and it was then concluded that mileage earning less than average cost was running at a loss. This of course excluded contributory revenue – earnings above inescapable cost – and gave rise to the concept of an 'unremunerative' service, which Ponsonby was later to rebut (Ponsonby, 1963).

The outcome of all this was nothing short of disastrous. While many small firms whose owners were close enough to the market had an instinctive awareness of sensible costing, the larger firms, whether municipal, state-owned or private, set about the reduction of unremunerative mileage, which as a consequence spread fixed costs over a smaller output and thereby increased average cost per mile. Then at the next review mileage would be cut still more. The process continued, seemingly unchallenged, for a further 30 years and more, just as car use and ownership were growing exponentially, and the ending of price control in 1980 had little immediate effect. What had happened might well be described as *the strange suicide of the British bus industry*.

Restructuring

Many smaller businesses were acquired by BTC companies, but the return of a Conservative majority in 1951 brought this to a standstill, while the Transport Act of 1953 did away with the powers of compulsory purchase, and wound up the executives. The Tilling Group management board and its equivalent in

Scotland were left alone to run their businesses, while the BTC concentrated on the growing problem of the railways. The bus industry was already starting to run into financial difficulties, to which the general response was withdrawal from the 'thin rural' areas and the growing but little understood practice of cross-subsidy. Passenger demand began to fall with the end of petrol rationing in 1950, and increasingly the competition of the private car was beginning to make itself felt, against the background of the costing errors which we have already examined.

The appointment in 1961 of Dr Richard Beeching to be the champion of the railways[1] led rapidly to the Transport Act of 1962, which abolished the British Transport Commission and set up the British Railways Board, but did little more for the bus industry than to transfer the BTC companies to a new Transport Holding Company. It was significant that individual operating companies continued to exist, while the continued independence of the BET companies meant that the area boundary agreements remained effective.[2] The cartel was to remain something more than an image. But loss-making rural services were becoming a problem, and in 1961 the Jack Committee[3] recommended subsidy; but no action was taken. A similar lack of interest marked the line closures arising from the first Beeching Report. Replacement bus services were usually subsidised by British Railways, but when the subsidy

1 *Beeching, Champion of the Railways?* was the title of a book by R. H. N. Hardy (Hardy, 1989). In his introduction Hardy, a former senior railway manager, says that Beeching 'saved the railways from financial and organisational disintegration'.

2 The BTC companies in England and Wales were subject to the strong centralising policy that had been typical of the Thomas Tilling group, contrary to the delegated management policy of British Electric Traction.

3 *Report of the Committee on Rural Bus Services*. Similar reports were made for the Highlands and Islands and for Wales.

expired they generally ceased to run, often because the demand had fallen away in any case. Destinations no longer served by rail disappeared from railway timetables and advertising in what was a notable example of the failure of the coordination that had been expected under the Transport Act 1947.

Meanwhile the growth of car ownership and use continued to expand, something that neither railway nor bus managers appear to have taken into account. The management of the industry was no longer in the hands of businessmen for whom such matters as return on capital or revenue maximisation were of central importance. The car was not seen as a competitor, but rather as a parallel industry. Public transport was coming to be seen by management as a matter of running trains and buses, rather than carrying people or goods in the wider market, and by politicians as a utility. The existence of price control and the absence of shareholders may be seen as the background to what was to continue to be the strange suicide of the British bus industry, while the case for reform of the 1930 act (see Hibbs, 1963) was ignored.

Following a change of government in 1964, Dr Beeching resigned, but his reforms continued. In due course Barbara Castle became Minister of Transport, and there followed a series of White Papers, leading to the Transport Act 1968, which changed many things. The state-owned bus services were transferred to a new National Bus Company (NBC) and a Scottish Transport Group,[4] each of which retained subsidiary operating companies with traditional titles, though it is uncertain how far their finances were distinct. At the same time the British Electric Traction board

4 It has been suggested that the NBC was originally to have been the National Bus Group, but the initials (standing also for No Bloody Good) would have been unfortunate.

reached the conclusion that bus operation was no longer financially attractive, so the NBC acquired the former BET companies, which were in due course 'Tillingised'. The area traffic commissioners' powers remained unchanged, and average cost pricing continued to be pursued. For the longer term the act made provision for subsidy as a matter of policy, and in the following years it was widely taken up by the new Passenger Transport Executives, whose managers were thus relieved of the need to consider the principles of costing.

Even more significant was the creation under this act of four area Passenger Transport Authorities (PTAs).[5] The White Paper *Public Transport and Traffic* of 1966 observed that land-use planning policy was not integrated with the management of public transport, especially in urban conditions, and included a proposal for new 'Conurbation Transport Authorities', designed to bring the two functions together. At the time it did not seem that they would be given operating powers, but when Richard Marsh, as Barbara Castle's successor, introduced the bill each PTA was to be responsible for a Passenger Transport Executive (PTE), which would acquire the transport undertakings of all municipalities in their area, with power to specify the services of any other operators, and to enter into agreements with British Rail. The members of each authority were nominated by the local authorities concerned, together with two more appointed by the minister. Several councils objected to the scheme, on the basis of municipal pride and of the contribution of surplus revenue to their accounts. Perhaps more significant was the way each new

5 They were for Merseyside, South-East Lancashire & North-East Cheshire ('SELNEC'), Tyneside and the West Midlands. A PTA for Greater Glasgow was created in 1972.

PTE came to follow the policies of the strongest council business in its area (see Box 3).

Box 3 Empire-building

The West Midlands PTE acquired the fleets of Birmingham City Council and of Walsall, West Bromwich and Wolverhampton, each with different policies, practices and loyalties. It was unfortunate that the choice of livery for the new fleet was close to the former Birmingham style and colour, and there was considerable public resentment. The new management moved quickly to do away with the old liveries, and to close down the Wolverhampton trolleybus system. The Local Government Act of 1972 transferred the Coventry municipal fleet to the PTE in 1974, much to the disapproval of Coventry Corporation. The PTE also acquired the operations of the former BET operator in its area, Midland 'Red'.

The scheme was designed with local government reform in mind, but it was to be 1974 before the Local Government Act 1972 created metropolitan counties, and defined them as PTAs. The new councils had extended areas, bringing additional municipal fleets into the PTEs, while the formation of South Yorkshire and West Yorkshire created two more PTAs. Membership of the PTAs changed, removing the minister's direct appointments, with the consequence that they tended from then on to be more politically slanted, while the subsequent concentration of Labour control in their areas introduced what may be called socialist policies for the

PTEs, using subsidy to maintain the existing networks and to hold down fares. Furthermore, when the Conservatives did away with the metropolitan county councils, the PTAs remained in existence, their members nominated now by the largely Labour-controlled unitary councils.

By the time the Labour government approached the election of 1979, passenger transport in the metropolitan counties can be said to have been brought within the Geddes philosophy. The quantity licensing that commenced with the Road Traffic Act 1930 continued to apply, subject to the requirement that the traffic commissioners upheld the decisions of the PTEs. Fares were still endorsed on the Road Service Licence. The quality licences remained, except that the 1968 act required the issue of an operator's licence, reflecting recent EU legislation. The act had also provided for subsidy, on the grounds that it was needed to retain rural bus services, but in the outcome it was directed to a much greater extent to the PTEs. Most important for the prosperity of the industry, the use of average cost criteria remained largely unchanged, leading to extended subsidy in the conurbations and the growth of similar support in rural areas.

Why, then, was subsidy so rapidly increased after 1968, and how far is it still assumed to be proper government policy for the bus industry? The Jack Report (see above) had recommended subsidy for rural services, and the Buchanan Report, *Traffic in Towns*, had argued for a more prominent role for public transport, which would seem to imply financial support. Subsidy was seen to be acceptable for the railways. Integration was now coming to be a popular term, replacing the 'coordination' of the inter-war years. The policy of management was turning to the use of high-capacity vehicles, without conductors, and subsidy was seen to be justified to introduce 'one person operation'.[6] But it may well have been that the industry wanted less worry, and the money offered an easy way out. Satisfying the customer had ceased to be a serious objective for management in the bus industry until a certain element of rethinking began to appear in the late 1970s. Certainly in the metropolitan counties the left-dominated PTAs encouraged their executives to provide what was thought to be good for the public.

Summary – freedom or franchise?

The general sub-Keynesian thinking of the post-war years took little interest in transport, assuming that the industry was a utility suited for top-down management and control. The Geddes philosophy that had been enshrined in the nationalisation of 1947 was expected to produce the 'coordination' that remained the buzzword of the day. By 1962 the failure of such a policy had been demonstrated, but the potential of leaving market demand with commercial management and pricing to provide a solution was still unthinkable. Alongside the objective of a planned economy the importance of land-use planning was to grow, though with little thought for the implications of public transport, let alone of the growth of car ownership and use. But the massive intervention of government in the business of running trains and buses was to be the characteristic of policy for 40 years after the end of the war, little challenged, other than by a notable Hobart Paper published by the IEA (Ponsonby, 1969).

6 In practice this often meant fewer, bigger buses to maintain the same number of seats per mile, despite the public preference for frequency. The return of competition was to make bus managers think again.

By the end of the 1970s there was a growing desire for more freedom among the younger managers in the National Bus Company, many of whom went on to make a success of privatisation. Arguments for franchise were less often to be heard, although such a policy could be recognised in many other countries. Only the small businesses in the coaching trade continued with no more than safety regulation. In general it was 'government knows best'.

It is, however, open to debate as to how far the licensing system introduced in 1931 and continued despite public ownership of much of the industry after 1945 was in effect a form of franchise. I have argued elsewhere (Hibbs, 1985: 267–70) that a division exists between a regulatory or a franchise approach to public transport and that, in general, a distinction can be made between the Anglo-Saxon attitude to be seen in Britain, the USA and the 'old Commonwealth countries'[7] and that of the European continent and other parts of the world, reflecting perhaps the opposing views of Locke and Descartes. In so far as the contradictions lie between arbitration and franchise, the British system may lean more to the former, but by 1979 the difference probably did not matter a great deal. Freedom to manage a transport business on commercial lines had largely expired.

7 My research presented in that text suggested that franchise was less common in South American countries, owing no doubt to the influence of British and American investment there.

3 DEREGULATION AND PRIVATISATION – UP TO A POINT

Time for a change

After the 1979 election the new government under Margaret Thatcher set out to restore the market, and while the bus industry was high on the list for reform, the process was carried out very carefully, step by step. The Transport Act 1980, introduced by Norman Fowler (which also included the final privatisation of the National Freight Corporation), made the first move. While this included some changes to safety regulation and enforced the requirement for a public service vehicle (PSV) operator's licence, the road service licence, issued by the traffic commissioners since 1930, was retained, though now only for the provision of a 'local service'. This meant that no such licence was required for an express service, with over 30 miles between stops, or for any 'excursion or tour'. The commissioners were now required to issue a road service licence to any applicant, 'unless they were satisfied that to do so would be against the interest of the public', thereby shifting the burden of proof from the applicant to the objector. Cautiously, the act went farther than this by removing price control as a condition of the licence for local services, subject to certain residual powers, which were never used.

The measure that was expected to open new doors to competition and to deal with the problem of loss-making rural bus services was the provision for 'trial areas', within which no road service licence would be required. This was set out in more detail in the Public Passenger Vehicles Act 1981, and it enabled county councils to ask for such an area to be set up, though there seems to have been no great enthusiasm for them. After pressure from the ministry four areas were designated, but only one, surrounding the city of Hereford, saw any lively response. There, after head-to-head competition for services offering little profitability, there eventually remained a single operator and continuing subsidy, and it was widely expected that this showed contestability and competition to be unworkable. In the express sector of the market there was a short-lived outbreak of competition, which the state-owned operators saw off quite quickly, reducing some of their cross-country services which they claimed to have cross-subsidised, but while there was price competition in that part of the market there is little evidence to suggest that the bus companies took advantage of their freedom where local services were concerned.

The Public Passenger Vehicles Act also redefined bus and coach services for licensing purposes, and extended the safety and quality regulations. In 1982 a further act presented by David Howell privatised the express and holiday services of the National Bus Company. While regulations continued to expand, reform was still not on the horizon when the Local Government Finance Act of 1982 brought the operations of the Passenger Transport Executives (PTEs) into the control of government audit, thus reducing their freedom to take commercial decisions involving risk. There followed a White Paper, *Public Transport Subsidy in Cities*, and a Commons inquiry which led to the Transport Act 1983, giving government power to make 'guidelines' for the size of public transport subsidy in the metropolitan counties and in London.

The PTEs were authorised to put services out for commercial tender, bringing the concept of franchise for the first time on to the agenda. In the meantime the use of bus services in the UK continued to decline.

In June 1983 the Conservatives were returned to power for a second term, and in October Nicholas Ridley became Secretary of State for Transport. Deregulation now came to be expected, and resistance to it rapidly appeared and grew. In less than a year from his appointment Ridley had prepared a White Paper, simply called *Buses*, which set out his intentions for reform.[1] It remains a striking document, arguing plainly for the return of the industry to the market, along with the restriction of subsidy. Well aware of the opposition coming from the leading figures in the industry, including independent operators as well as those in the nationalised and municipal sector, Ridley wasted no time in presenting the bill, which was to become the Transport Act 1985, receiving royal assent on 30 October.

Ridley's arguments were received with reservation in many quarters. In a valuable and well-informed study of the industry (Savage, 1985), one writer concluded that 'unfettered competition' was undesirable, and advocated short-term franchising or contracting of bus services, presenting the case for competition *for* the market instead of *in* the market, which as we shall see was to reappear in the Transport Act 2000. Opposition to the bill was offset by support from many of the younger managers in the industry, who had been frustrated by the centralising policies of

1 The White Paper (Cmnd. 9300) is a remarkable document and well worth returning to. It sets out the argument for a competitive industry in a very readable form, and includes appendices on 'The Scope for Improved Efficiency' and 'Cross-subsidisation in Stage Bus Operations' which are strongly recommended for reading today.

the National Bus Company (NBC). It is true to say that the NBC was turning to a more market-oriented policy as early as 1981, when the large Midland 'Red' company was divided into four to enable a more 'hands-on' management style. No approval came from the politicised Passenger Transport Authorities or their bureaucratic executives, and the remaining municipal operators were similarly opposed, while the trade unions, as was to be expected, were strongly critical.

While the White Paper made the case for a generally commercial industry outside London, in the act the work of the parliamentary draftsmen inevitably produced a much more complex picture. The belief so often heard that Ridley 'deregulated the bus industry' is an oversimplification, and it would be better to refer to regulatory reform, along with privatisation, as the outcome of the statute. While it might be expected that a regulatory authority responsible for the 'quality' issues such as safety of vehicles and drivers would be needed, the area traffic commissioners were retained not just for that purpose, but with significant residual powers of control.

At the heart of the matter the road service licence, which since the 1980 act had continued to regulate local services, except for the fares, was replaced by the registration of local bus services, with the exception of those in London and any provided for railway replacement. It was to be necessary for an application for registration to be approved by the traffic commissioner, and there was to be a 'period of notice' before the service could commence, with a further period before the service could be varied or cancelled. Clearly these limitations on contestability showed a fear of hit-and-run competition, perhaps fuelled by the experience of the Hereford trial area.

The other controversial element in the bill was the disposal of the National Bus Company, or, in other words, privatisation. Part III of the act provided for this in some detail, making it clear that it was the subsidiary companies which were to be disposed of. Critics now suggested that competition should take place 'off and not on the street'. In an internal paper, *Problems with Franchising*, dated March 1985 (seen by this author), the Economics Directorate of the department examined the arguments for franchising in some detail and identified serious problems. Its summary commences as follows: 'Franchising appears to offer the benefits of competition without the effort of its actual practice. However, experience shows that much of this promise is illusory: there are various types of "frictions" in the process. The contractual disabilities can be quite severe. The problems exist whether or not the franchise is for a natural monopoly.' The two most serious problems are stated to be the element of protection given to the incumbent, and the substantial monopoly power that is provided. These words are highly relevant in terms of today's pressure from the Passenger Transport Executive Group (PTEG) for 'quality contracts', which are in effect a franchise, and the paper must have influenced the eventual design of the Transport Bill. The act retained the Passenger Transport Authorities, however, which continued to exist when the powers of the metropolitan counties were substantially returned to the boroughs.

What happened next?

The secretary of state now proceeded to issue regulations under which the 'deregulation' was to proceed. They provided for a transitional period to commence on 6 January 1986, during which various dates were set for the registration of services and for changes in registration. 'Deregulation Day' was to be 26 October 1986, but this was to be followed by an 'initial period', a freeze of all the registrations received. The process ended on 26 January 1987, after which 42 calendar days' notice was required for variations, cancellations and new registrations, subject to the traffic commissioner's discretion to allow shorter periods.[2] Now the fun was to begin.

The first years of the new regime saw some fairly drastic examples of what could fairly be described as misuse of the new freedom, with some small firms being put out of business by larger competitors who could afford to charge no fares, making up their losses afterwards. In Darlington a Stagecoach subsidiary, having failed to agree a price to acquire the municipally owned company (see below), drove it out of business by running free buses just in front of the company's. On the other hand there were many examples of small firms coming into the market with lower costs and attracting substantial business from the larger operators, a notable case being found in Greater Manchester. The Darlington episode was subsequently investigated by the Monopolies and Mergers Commission, and there was an element of bad publicity surrounding the early days of competition, not least because several of the larger firms do not seem to have been well prepared for the outcome. The Office of Fair Trading examined a number of cases of alleged predatory pricing, but came across very few cases where it could be proved.[3]

2 The act did away with the provision for local authorities to nominate members to a panel of commissioners, the chairman at that time becoming a single commissioner.

3 See 'An Introduction to Competition Legislation', contributed by the Office of Fair Trading to *Your Guide to the 1985 Transport Act*, Transport Publishing

The act required the privatisation of the National Bus Company (NBC) within three years, with the approval of the secretary of state and of HM Treasury; the latter, it may be assumed, sought the maximum income from the process. It has been suggested that this could have been in conflict with the objective of increased competition resulting from reducing the size of the companies.[4] What followed was the sale of the NBC companies as going concerns. The subsequent years saw the businesses that had been acquired by management or managers and staff sold, with a few exceptions, to the growing ownership groups. The outcome of this has been the reappearance of the pre-war cartel, in practice if not in form, for while the act ended the exemption of bus operators from the Restrictive Trade Practices Act and made the pre-nationalisation 'area agreements' illegal, there can be little doubt that informal 'understandings' have continued to exist. Cross-border competition between large firms has been very rare. On the other hand there is a continuing problem where operators find it difficult to obtain approval for common fares on services operated jointly.

With regard to local government interests the act required the bus operations of each of the PTEs to be transferred to a company limited by shares, owned by either the PTE or its PTA. These were to be broken down into smaller units so as to encourage competition, such as was the intention for the NBC breakdown. This never happened, and the PTE companies remained substantial in size. The consequences varied from one area to another, with the West Midlands PTE, West Midlands Travel, financially successful while on the other hand its Greater Manchester equivalent found

Projects, Cardiff, 1986.

4 See *Your Guide to the 1985 Transport Act*, op. cit., p. 44.

it necessary to cut a great deal of mileage, owing, it seems, to a failure to understand its own costs. In subsequent years all these companies were sold to one or other of the ownership groups, the Greater Manchester business being divided into two for the purpose.

Municipal operators were subject to similar provisions. Each district council with a transport undertaking was required to submit a scheme for the approval of the secretary of state, with joint proposals permitted, for transfer of the property concerned to a municipally owned company. An operating subsidy would not be allowed, but there was no requirement to show a profit. Under some pressure, the majority of these businesses were sold, subject to the purchaser not being an operator in the surrounding area, leaving seventeen still formally owned by local councils.

The sale of the individual NBC companies and the PTE operations meant that territorial boundaries, some of them established as far back as 1916, remained in existence. It is hard to see how this achieved the expectation of the White Paper in restoring the industry to the market. Some commentators still find it hard to tolerate untidiness and are also intolerant of the smaller firms that come and go 'snapping at the heels' of the larger businesses, reminiscent of the 'pirates' of the 1920s, who were condemned for serving only the peak, while the 'responsible' operators had to 'bear the heat and burden of the day'. That argument had long since been refuted by Ponsonby (1958), who showed that the larger firms benefited from such competition by needing fewer vehicles, of which a high proportion had to remain idle throughout the greater part of the day.

The reaction of the industry to its new freedom was restrained. After a study sponsored by the Department for Transport and

Birmingham Polytechnic Business School (Hibbs, 1991), this author concluded that the legislation of 1980 and 1985 was 'having the effect of making a formerly product-driven industry learn to adjust to the requirements of the market', but that it still had some way to go. These developments were examined in more detail in another study (Hibbs and Bradley, 1996), which stressed the need for further change, but recognised that the 'managed decline' of the industry appeared to have come to an end. Central to this had been the practice of standard costing, comparing average revenue per mile with average cost per mile, inherited, as we have seen, from the regulators in the 1950s and enforced thereafter under statute, which took a decade or more to disappear; indeed, it may be that some operators subscribe to it still. A group of senior managers interviewed by this author in 1996–99[5] suggested that awareness of the market had come to be understood to some extent. All agreed about the importance of marketing, but the group was divided 50–50 on the subject of price discrimination, which had become a possibility as early as 1980. What has happened has been the *simplification* of pricing, with a standard fare over wide areas, directed to make bus use easier, though this has been offset by the refusal of many of the larger companies to allow drivers to give change. Reduced fares at certain times for pensioners came from local government subsidy, unlike the well-established policy of British Rail, which was designed to attract demand outside the peak with no element of subsidy. Pre-payment schemes have provided for regular passengers, frequently in response to competition from smaller firms with lower fares, but outright price competition has been

5 Research funded by the Rees Jeffreys Road Fund.

rare, and marketing by price remains less common than it is in the supermarket sector, for example.

The same managers were asked to assess the general attitude of the industry to some relevant issues in the post-deregulation world. First was the importance of the Office of Fair Trading, which had extended its concern to the buses in 1985. Here there was an equal division between those who saw the industry's attitude as positive and those who saw it as negative. All agreed that 'marketing management' was seen to be important, and much the same was felt with regard to costing, but the conclusion remains that serious marketing effort has taken a long time to emerge from the liberalisation of the industry (see Hibbs, 1998, with special reference to London). A recent comment from outside could perhaps throw some light on this. The chief executive of Translink, the Northern Ireland state bus company, suggested that if privatisation had happened first, then bus operators would have had an easier time with deregulation.[6]

Where are we now?

Throughout its history the bus industry has been marked by a tendency towards concentration of ownership. Economies of scale, which should have encouraged businessmen to expand the territory of their operations, were limited by the existence of municipal tramway departments, which started to run buses themselves at an early date. Each territory seems to have been limited by diseconomies arising from distance, so that as ownership groups appeared their operating units remained discrete,

6 Quoted in the magazine *Bus and Coach Professional*, 18 March 2005.

with trading names directed at customer loyalty. Definitions of territorial boundaries, the legally unchallenged 'area agreements',[7] led to the emergence of the cartel in 1916 and thereafter. The larger municipalities benefited also from economies of scale, disposing of surpluses either by way of subsidy or by reducing their citizens' rates. At least two had area agreements with their neighbouring companies.

While the large firm can take advantage of discounts for fuel and spare parts and choose between competing suppliers for investment in vehicles, it may also suffer from diseconomies of large scale which its smaller competitors escape. While many of the small firms that emerged after 1919 sold out when licensing in 1931 gave them a valuable monopoly, or again when nationalisation began after 1947, it is in the nature of the trade that a manager closer to the market and free to initiate can prosper where the remoteness of management in the large business may be a serious disadvantage. Thus the centralised top-down style of the Tilling Group, which was passed on to the National Bus Company in due course, undoubtedly contributed to the 'strange suicide of the British bus industry' which we have remarked upon already. What is most notable is the structure of what may be called 'the coaching trade': the numerous small firms, often family businesses, which remain in both urban and rural areas, providing for private customers hiring their vehicles, offering excursions and tours, tendering for contracts of various kinds, including subsidised bus services, and sometimes engaging also in the licensed minicab trade.

7 These agreements were almost certainly contracts in restraint of trade, but none of the parties had any incentive to challenge them.

Such firms remain small,[8] and may come and go as the state of the market or family concerns make for change.

Many of the former NBC and Scottish Bus Group companies were disposed of through management or management/staff buyouts. The industry was no longer exempt from competition law so the territorial area agreements were now illegal, but they had continued to exist by default under state ownership, and they remain informally in existence today. Before long the trend towards consolidation reappeared, and today there are now five PLCs which are holding companies, and four smaller groups. A number of these operate services franchised by Transport for London, while some have operations in other European countries. Several of the PLCs also hold rail franchises as train operating companies. Alongside these there are very many smaller firms (the 'independents'), some with their own small 'territory' and others running on the routes of their larger competitors.

Standards of service have varied over the past twenty years, and the more successful groups have delegated management to their subsidiaries, while others have been faced with serious problems, due perhaps to too much top-down control. More recently the larger companies have invested large sums in greatly improved vehicles, encouraged by new statutory requirements for disabled access, but in some areas the smaller firms have been able to operate at competitive fares by using elderly and more basic buses, something that has tended to bring the industry into disrepute. On the other hand the smaller groups

8 From personal experience and observation, the present author concludes that expansion beyond a fleet size of between 20 and 40 vehicles will lead to inefficiencies of scope which can only be overcome by seeking rapid growth with a more formal structure.

and many of the independents have made considerable advances in customer care, with incentives for drivers to work as part of the team.

The amount of on-street competition expected by some of those who advocated deregulation in the 1980s has been limited. It became plain that consolidation would be limited by the Office of Fair Trading so that something like the pre-1947 territorial structure has remained in effect. The smaller firms continue snapping at the heels of the larger urban operators, tending to hold down fares, but while a successful marketing drive has emerged in more recent years in some of the companies, in others there are signs that the 'strange suicide' continues. Quite recently there has been a spurt of competition for longer-distance services on main corridors, with online booking and sophisticated pricing policies encouraging growth.

Summary – freedom or franchise?

It took a long time for the bus and coach industry to adjust to the extended commercial freedom provided by the Transport Acts of 1980 and 1985. This may be accounted for by two factors: the resettlement period as the ownership and management of the industry reacted to change, and the inherited reliance on average costing and pricing dating back to the intervention of the traffic commissioners in the early 1950s. The concept of passenger transport as a utility suited for centralised public control goes back to the thoughts of men like Geddes and Ashfield a century ago. Attempts to apply this to the movement of freight were shown to fail, but whereas the ownership pattern of that industry remains significantly small-scale, there are still economies of scale in bus transport which account for the larger businesses that have always existed and have always sought to combine.

What we have seen more recently has been the reappearance of the Geddes philosophy, with a marked political slant. Whereas it was once possible to argue that utilities were best held in public ownership, a line of reasoning that produced the London Passenger Transport Board in 1933 and the nationalisation of 1947, more recent history has shown that 'commercial' management is less wasteful of resources, for reasons that public choice theory makes plain. As a compromise we are now told that competition may not be a bad thing, but it must be 'competition *for* the market', not 'competition *in* the market'. This idea, commonly found in other parts of the world, is now put forward by the left-leaning Passenger Transport Executives and was supported by the Labour Party, the Liberal Democrats and the Green Party in the recent general election.

It is easily refuted as false logic. Competition is what goes on *in* a market. What the argument really proposes is competition *for a monopoly*. To prevent exploitation of such a monopoly, the franchise must be for a limited period of time, after which the auction will be held again. A consequence of this is the loss of investment suffered by a company that fails to renew its franchise, which was provided for in rail privatisation by the leasing of rolling stock. But in Britain today the successful franchisee in the bus industry is not intended to be a fully commercial monopolist at all.

4 WHO SHALL RUN THE BUSES?

The politics of franchise

The latest government intervention, the Transport Act 2000, was a monumental intrusion into the freedom of transport management in Britain: 107 sections dealt with air traffic, 27 with road user charging and the workplace parking levy, 53 with railways and 54 with local transport. Then there were 25 'Miscellaneous and Supplementary' sections and 31 schedules, mostly about the railways. Weighing 880 grams, it was by far the heaviest document in a series that had steadily increased in size and weight ever since 1921. Seen at the time to incorporate a move to the re-regulation of the bus industry, it set the course for decision-making to be taken over by 'public choice' – that is, in the political market place rather than in the market for bus users.

The act opened the door to re-regulation, giving local government opportunities, under state supervision, to impose, first, *quality partnerships*, and then, if they were not satisfied, *quality contracts*. The quality contract would be a European-style franchise. These approaches clearly reflect the fact that the Geddes philosophy of 1919 is still alive and kicking. Commercial freedom would be constrained by quality partnerships, and abolished by the quality contracts. Far from being quality licensing as discussed above, they were designed to impose, first, *quantity control*, and then *price control*. The relevant sections are as follows, with a brief comment in each case. Unlike most of the previous legislation that we have discussed, the act did not apply to Scotland.

In Sections 108 and 109 the act set up 'Local Transport Authorities' (LTAs), which are county councils and Passenger Transport Authorities (PTAs) in England, and county or borough councils in Wales (the PTAs are not directly elected bodies). Each LTA is required to 'develop policies for the promotion and encouragement of *safe, integrated, efficient and economic transport facilities and services*' (emphasis added), to be called 'Local Transport Plans'. No attempt is made to define what is meant by 'integrated', 'efficient' or 'economic', and so we start with the utmost freedom for politicians to decide what transport facilities and services might be; it is hard to imagine a more serious departure from economic rigour. All that is expected is set out in Section 110, under which each LTA must prepare a 'Bus Strategy' to meet 'the transport requirements of such persons as the LTA consider should be met by such services', at 'the standards that the LTA consider should be provided', however these standards are to be defined and measured. There is no mention at this stage of discussing the strategy with the businesses already active in the market.

This comes with the next stage. Sections 114 to 123 enable an LTA, or two or more LTAs, to make a 'quality partnership scheme'. This is to be mostly about 'facilities', but it may include 'requirements which the vehicles being used … must meet'. Just what these facilities are is not made clear, but the scheme may not include 'requirements as to the frequency or timing of the services'. This time the LTA must consult operators of services concerned, organisations representing users of local services, the appropriate traffic commissioner and the chief police officer. Notice must be given to all operators of local services likely to be affected. What this means is a mutual agreement between the LTA and some or all of the local bus companies to work together regarding highway improvements and bus shelters, and the like, and operating standards, such as the choice of vehicles.

Such a scheme seems to be a kind of quid pro quo between operators and the local authority, but the next step is very much more hostile to the liberty of management in running buses for commercial ends. Under Sections 124 and 125 an LTA (or two or more LTAs) may make a 'quality contract scheme' if they are satisfied that 'this is the only practicable way of implementing the policies set out in their bus strategy'. Under such a scheme the LTA will be able to 'determine what local services are to be provided ... and any additional facilities or services which should be provided'. A quality contract is then defined as an agreement under which the LTA 'grant[s] to another person the exclusive right to operate the local services to which the contract relates' and 'that person undertakes to provide the services on such terms (including in particular terms relating to *frequency, fares and standards of service*) as may be specified in the agreement' (emphasis added). Consultations are required as for a partnership scheme, with the additional proviso that all operators in the area of the scheme must be included, after which modifications may be proposed, and under Sections 126–129 the LTA must apply to 'the appropriate national authority' for approval of the scheme. Finally, the LTA is required to invite tenders for the contract, for a period not exceeding five years (Sections 130–132), and a scheme may be varied or revoked if 'the conditions are no longer met'. A tender may only be accepted from a person who holds either a Public Service Vehicle Operator's Licence or a Community Bus Permit, and the traffic commissioner must be notified when a contract is entered into. Various regulations are provided for in Sections 133 and 134.

The politics of intervention – again

The Passenger Transport Executives Group (PTEG) has from its formation pressed for the return of bus services to public control by franchise (see Hibbs, 1998). It will be remembered that the Passenger Transport Authorities after 1974 had been made up of councillors nominated by the Labour-controlled local authorities in their area. The quality contracts provided for in the Transport Act 2000 provide for their political intent, while the quality partnerships form a halfway house, in fact largely acceptable by the industry, which has remained firmly opposed to the contracts.[1] Political pressure for the further development of franchise was reflected in the proposals of the political parties in the 2005 general election, limited as their interest in the industry appeared to be.

When the Transport Act 2000 was being prepared there appeared from the European Commission a Draft Regulation 'on action by Member States concerning public service requirements and the award of public service contracts in passenger transport by rail, road and inland waterway' (for details see Hibbs, 2003). Very close in design to the quality contracts, the regulation would require a 'competent authority' to 'pursue legitimate public service objectives within a framework of regulated competition'.

1 When Coventry City Council persuaded the West Midlands PTE to impose a quality contract the major local operator settled for a quality partnership, with new vehicles and rebranding.

While this may seem to some to be reasonable, it looks very different when the required criteria are considered (see Box 4 – the clauses that follow contain still more bureaucratic detail for page after page); the 'competent authority' would be controlling every detail of the operation within each five-year franchise. If managers had to spend so much of their time satisfying the 'competent authority' they would have little time left to consider the demands of the market. Above all, price control would weaken the economic efficiency of the operator and lead inevitably to the waste of resources, quite apart from the growing cost of subsidy, which is to be seen in the London system of franchise.

The pressure for quality contracts comes largely from the PTEs, most of which have an interest in the provision of Light Rapid Transit (LRT). Because trams are to be found in Continental cities it would seem that their absence in Britain shows us to be falling behind. Yet almost all the investment in LRT in this country has been loss-making, imposing a greater burden on council tax. It is as if the tradition of municipal pride in the tramway back in the twentieth century has resurfaced in the political fashion that has led to so much waste, with too many examples of poor forecasting and design. Yet it is the PTEs themselves which have been responsible, and it this that contributes a further strand to their pressure for franchise.

Almost all the existing LRT lines in this country use reserved track, often disused railway lines, but there are schemes afoot for on-street running which would bring the trams and buses into direct competition. In such cases it is common on the Continent for the bus services to be curtailed so as to direct demand to the trams, which cost so much more to provide. Buses are expected to act as feeders to the trams, despite the disadvantage for the customer of having to change from one to the other. It is hard

Box 4 The European Union plans for franchise

Article 48, Clause 2 of the proposed EU regulation required the authority to take into account 'at least the following criteria':

- consumer protection factors including the accessibility of services in terms of their frequency, speed, punctuality, reliability, the extent of the network and the service information that is provided;
- the level of tariffs for different groups of users and the transparency of tariffs;
- integration between different transport services, including integration of information, ticketing, timetables, consumer rights and the use of interchanges;
- accessibility for people with reduced mobility;
- environmental factors, including local, national and international standards for the emission of air pollutants, noise and global warming gases;
- the balanced development of regions;
- transport needs of people living in less densely populated areas;
- passenger health and safety;
- the qualifications of staff; and
- how complaints are handled, disputes between passengers and operators are resolved and redress is made for service shortfalls.

to avoid the conclusion, then, that quality contracts would be so devised as to do the same, sweeping both modes into one 'integrated' system, whether the customers want it or not. Perhaps this is what that overused word means. In the 1930s it was 'coordination', which would have meant much the same thing.

Summary – freedom or franchise?

In 2003 the Passenger Transport Authorities set out their vision for the future.[2] They would be able to specify 'integrated routes, timetables, network tickets and fares, with emphasis on the social, environmental and economic importance of bus services rather than the profit motive'. They would remove wasteful 'on the road' competition 'which uses up valuable resources'. They would operate a bus service 'of last resort' where commercial bus operators cannot or will not operate a service, and they would make sure that public finance and subsidies 'are used in the most effective manner'. Finally, they would lease buses to smaller bus companies. Given a quality contract or an EU-style structure, this is what they would do. The director of the PTE Group's Support Unit is quoted as saying that 'there would be a net gain of up to £150m' if quality contracts were introduced over all the PTE areas, adding that there would be increased subsidy. 'Cost I believe will be higher because quality does cost,' he is reported to have said.[3]

It is hard to conceive of a policy for public transport, short of total public ownership, that takes us farther from the benefits that follow from an open and contestable market. And it is hard to see how capable, imaginative and risk-taking managers would remain

2 As reported in *Transit* magazine, 4 July 2003.

3 ibid., 26 November 2004.

in the bus industry under such constraints. Geddes and Ashfield would no doubt have approved, but who, it must be asked, could have the information, the insight or the wisdom to apply such a policy to a complex industry, and thereby to satisfy the demand of people who know best for themselves what level and quality of service it is that they are prepared to pay for? And how are we to be protected from wasteful bureaucratic procedures, diverting funds from the provision of services, open to the impact of the vote motive and averse to risk? For these are the problems arising inescapably from top-down public control such as this.

After twenty years of comparative freedom the bus industry today has become a commercial success. Despite failings in some sectors there are many examples of proactive response to the market, with increased investment and some remarkable developments in man-management and consumer sensitivity. The central importance of costing and pricing for the market has been better understood than ever before and the provision of real-time information is making a new breakthrough in marketing. Some of the small firms snapping at the heels of the larger companies provide poor-quality vehicles which give a poor impression to the public, but the value of open access is recognised by some of the leading figures in the industry, while many small operators offer a high standard of customer care along with lower prices. While the overall proportion of bus travel continues to fall, there are many examples of substantial growth; restructuring of services in Cambridge has led to an increase in patronage of 45 per cent over three years.

What has been sadly lacking ever since 1985 has been a positive attitude on the part of highway authorities. To provide services buses need their own track, like trains. This has to be shared with cars and goods vehicles, but cars are singularly inefficient users of road space and in the absence of road pricing it should be the responsibility of local government to deal with the problem. Buses, however, do not rank high in public status, and motorists, who are voters and ratepayers, resent the introduction of bus lanes and other kinds of priority. A professional gap seems to have grown between urban planners and bus operators, reflecting perhaps a distrust of commercial management. After the Transport Act 2000 the quality partnerships were designed to overcome this, but there now seems to be a real possibility that franchise would simply make things worse, by throwing the baby out with the bath water.

The real problem facing the passenger and freight transport industry, whether by bus, car or train, is the prospect of falling overall motoring costs and rising fuel prices forecast over the coming decade. Subsidy, which is an inevitable consequence of franchise, can be no answer to this. Only an industry made up of professional, profit-seeking businesses can hope to meet the challenge, supported and respected by local government planners. In that way Nicholas Ridley's vision for buses can yet be made a reality, and the 'Geddes philosophy' at last set aside. Let the first move be the revision of the Transport Act 2000, and an end to quality contracts.

References

Barker, T. and D. Gerhold (1993), *The Rise and Rise of Road Transport, 1700–1990*, London: Macmillan, 2nd edn.

Chester, D. N. (1936), *Public Control of Road Passenger Transport*, Manchester: Manchester University Press.

Hardy, R. H. N. (1989), *Beeching, Champion of the Railways?*, London: Ian Allan.

Hibbs, J. (1963), *Transport for Passengers*, London: Institute of Economic Affairs, Hobart Paper 23.

Hibbs, J. (1971), *Transport for Passengers*, London: Institute of Economic Affairs, Hobart Paper 23 (2nd, revised edn).

Hibbs, J. (1985), 'International comparisons of bus licensing', *Transport Reviews*, 6(3): 259–72.

Hibbs, J. (1989), *The History of British Bus Services*, Newton Abbot: David & Charles, 2nd edn.

Hibbs, J. (1991), 'An evaluation of urban bus deregulation in Britain: a survey of management attitudes', *Progress in Planning*, 36: 163–257.

Hibbs, J. (1998), *Trouble with the Authorities*, London: Adam Smith Institute.

Hibbs, J. (2003), *Running Buses: Who knows best what passengers want?*, London: Adam Smith Institute.

Hibbs, J. and M. Bradley (1996), *Deregulated Decade*, London: Adam Smith Institute.

Ponsonby, G. J. (1958), 'The problem of the peak, with special reference to road passenger transport', *Economic Journal*, LXVIII: 74ff.

Ponsonby, G. J. (1963), 'What is an unremunerative transport service?', *Journal of the Institute of Transport*, March, pp. 90ff.

Ponsonby, G. J. (1969), *Transport Policy: Co-ordination through Competition*, London, Institute of Economic Affairs, Hobart Paper 49.

Savage, C. (1985), *An Economic History of Transport*, London: Hutchinson.

Yelton, M. (2004), *Trams and Buses and the Law*, Brora: Adam Gordon.

PART 2: OTHER PERSPECTIVES ON MARKETS IN TRANSPORT

5 THE STATE CONTROL MESS

Eamonn Butler[1]

Introduction

For 50 years after 1930 the UK bus industry was a mess. It was a closely regulated system of route monopolists, with long-distance services dominated by the state-owned National Bus Company, and local services run by politically appointed bodies. Private enterprise was mostly confined to running small coach companies.

As a coach operator himself, John Hibbs saw that this regulation and state control made the bus industry grossly inefficient. As such, it was unable to compete with the rise of the private car. In 1957, some 34 per cent of all the miles travelled in Britain were by bus; 30 years later, it was only 8 per cent. Meanwhile the proportion of miles travelled in private vehicles doubled. Industry bosses saw this decay as inevitable. 'The policy of the 1960s and 1970s', wrote Hibbs, 'was one of managed decline.'

Worse, this shrinking industry had a growing appetite for taxpayer subsidies. As operating costs rose by 15–30 per cent above inflation in the decade 1972–82, state subsidies soared from £10 million in 1972 to £520 million ten years later! Clearly, this situation was unsustainable.

---

1 Eamonn Butler is director of the Adam Smith Institute.

Lessons from abroad

But looking around the world, it was clear that things could be different. Experts such as Hibbs's *Omega Project* co-authors Gabriel Roth and Anthony Shepherd (Adam Smith Institute, 1983), with practical experience of transport systems abroad, knew that competitive, entrepreneurial operators in other countries were seeing off the threat from cars and from cut-price state systems – by providing popular and effective alternatives.

Cairo's *jitneys*, for example, were minibuses operating on fixed routes, but to flexible timetables. They posted up a destination and then waited until they were full before setting off. A similar system operated in Jordan, and with Israel's shared inter-city *sheruts*. Istanbul had the *dolmus* (meaning 'stuffed'), which doubled as a conventional taxi as the need arose. In Manila there were the exotically decorated *jeepneys*, named after the US army jeep from which the originals were built. And in Buenos Aires, most people travelled on the *collectivos*, which began life in the 1920s as shared taxis, but grew into 25-seaters, a third of them owner-driven.

At a time when British transport planners were wedded to big buses running at long intervals, Hibbs and others saw that the owners and drivers of these small-scale competitive alternatives had a closer understanding of what their customers wanted, and could respond to it more quickly. Why could the same not happen here?

The courage to change

It could, of course, but it would take political determination to achieve it. Luckily, Mrs Thatcher's transport minister, Nicholas Ridley – a noted 'dry' – was up for the challenge. To shocked opposition from the incumbents, the transport quangos and local politicians – but bolstered by Hibbs's arguments (Hibbs, 1985 and elsewhere) – Ridley adopted the deregulation agenda wholesale. His 1985 Buses Act abolished the strict licensing system (except, sadly, in London).

Instantly, we started to see some of the vitality of the overseas, deregulated systems come to Britain: by the end of the first year alone, the number of long-distance services increased by a third. New routes sprang up where none had existed before. Fares fell, and customers switched from trains to buses that were often a tenth of the cost. And the National Bus Company, stripped of its monopoly protection, was broken up and sold off, just as Hibbs proposed in the *Omega Report*, mostly to management buyouts, which helped to extend the growth of competition still further.

Meanwhile, in the cities, competition and deregulation induced bus operators to provide customers with the services they actually wanted. Independent operators came forward to run new services, and tailored their fleets to meet demand – introducing minibuses, for example, on routes where more frequent services were demanded. New direct services sprang up: instead of passengers having to change buses and wait in windy bus stations, more direct services would take them across town, from point to point.

As Hibbs and co-author Matthew Bradley noted (1997), competition worked because operators suddenly had to understand and serve their customers to survive. New vehicles and proper staff training in customer care made the journey experience more pleasant. Buses even gained on cars in terms of popularity.

Competition and innovation had proved better than the old ideas of top-down 'integrated transport' policies. And with the spiral of decline and subsidy arrested, bus operations became profitable again, and in the process became large contributors to the Treasury, paying substantial sums in corporation tax, payroll taxes, fuel and other duties.

The unfinished agenda

Bus competition worked best, however, where the local authority worked constructively with the new private operators. Hibbs (1998) pointed to shining examples of this; but in other areas, he complained, local transport officials wanted to scrap deregulation and bring in highly regulated, European-style 'franchises'.

As in London, franchises would give the authorities complete control over fares, timetables, vehicles and routes (most of those, as Hibbs noted, having been established by the horse-bus associations of the nineteenth century). There would be little scope for operators to change their product in ways they believed would attract customers: 'There is nothing worse for a bus operator', he wrote, 'than to know that passengers are waiting in the rain because he is not allowed to deviate from some bureaucratically determined timetable' (Hibbs, 1999).

Hibbs was critical of the fact that the 1980s reforms actually deepened regulation in some areas, such as quality regulation, allowing local authorities to exert considerable power over private operators. The legislation could also have been better drafted to prevent predatory pricing, which may have driven out some fledgling operators. The goals of privatisation could have been clearer; and faster progress could have been made on the privatisation of municipally owned bus operations: 'The success of these companies, when they were eventually privatised, in quickly and effectively improving the quality of service has been remarkable, but it is unfortunate that it took so long to achieve' (ibid.).

The rise of road pricing

Another reform that has been a long time coming is road pricing. Hibbs was a keen supporter of the proposal, outlined in the 1964 Smeed Report (Ministry of Transport, 1964), and injected it into the 1983 *Omega Project*, pointing out that electronic schemes were now feasible. He continued to promote the idea with energy, in *Tomorrow's Way* (Roth and Hibbs, 1992), for example, which, like *Omega*, advocated a national highways trust to take over the management of the roads to depoliticise them and make sure that those who used them actually paid for them.

London now has a crude, paper-based congestion charging system, but electronic and other road pricing schemes now exist in many of the world's cities, where they have been found to cut congestion, promote a switch to public transport (not to mention cycling and walking), and generate large sums that can be invested in road and environmental improvements. Electronic schemes can also collect large amounts of traffic data which can be used to good effect in the management of traffic and to identify where new road investment is needed.

As well as cutting congestion, road pricing also cuts pollution, by enabling vehicles to drive at closer to optimal speeds instead of stopping and starting on overcrowded roads. It is also fairer. The Adam Smith Institute report *The Road from Inequity* suggested that under the current system of vehicle and fuel taxes, rural drivers pay three times too much for the modest congestion, pollution, noise, road damage and accidents they cause. By contrast, peak-time city car drivers pay one seventh of the amount they should pay, and peak-time lorry drivers only 1 per cent of the amount they should pay.

The current government, however, is committed to a road pricing system for lorries, and Transport Secretary Alistair Darling has indicated that a national road pricing system for all vehicles could be a possibility too. If it happens, it will be in no small part due to the dogged determination of John Hibbs in pushing the idea, in reports and seminars and with politicians, officials and transport bodies, over the course of some 30 years.

The debate continues

With politicians quite prepared to sacrifice sound economic principles for helpful headlines, we need such dogged and constant determination. In the 2005 Budget, for example, Chancellor Gordon Brown made a blatant appeal for the votes of Britain's 11 million pensioners by proposing free bus passes for them and for all disabled persons, beginning in April 2006.

Helping pensioners may be a laudable aim, but this policy, which extends what is already done in many local authorities, is an extension of bureaucratic intrusion into the transport market. It will muffle the system of price signals, which tell providers where their time and energy are best invested on behalf of their customers. No doubt the operators will be left to pick up the cost of the government's social policy, as other sectors such as the utilities have been. And it is untargeted: rich pensioners will reap the benefit, along with those in real need.

A better system, again outlined by Hibbs and his co-authors

in the *Omega Report*, would be national transport tokens. These can be focused solely on the individuals who are judged to need them. They can be used in any form of public transport – bus, tram, rail, taxi. The operators can then redeem them for cash. So the benefit goes to those who need it, and the market system is not disrupted.

From this, from the continuing debate on road pricing and from the attempts of local transport authorities to reassert their control through franchising, it is clear that the arguments for competition and markets are never won. They need to be stated and restated in response to each political intervention. The task needs clear thinking, good arguments, practical examples, courage and hands-on experience. It is the fact that John Hibbs has all those things in large measure which makes him such an important figure in the continuing history of transport policy.

References

Adam Smith Institute (1983), *Omega Project: Transport*, London: Adam Smith Institute.

Hibbs, J. (1985), *The Debate on Bus Deregulation*, London: Adam Smith Institute.

Hibbs, J. (1998), *Trouble with the Authorities*, London: Adam Smith Institute.

Hibbs, J. (1999), *Don't Stop the Bus*, London: Adam Smith Institute.

Hibbs, J. and M. Bradley (1997), *Deregulated Decade*, London: Adam Smith Institute.

Ministry of Transport (1964), *Road Pricing: The Economic and Technical Possibilities* (The Smeed Report), London: HMSO.

Pirie, M. (1980), *The Paratransit Light Vehicle*, London: Adam Smith Institute.

Roth, G. and J. Hibbs (1992), *Tomorrow's Way*, London: Adam Smith Institute.

Roth, G. and A. Shepherd (1984), *Wheels within Cities*, London: Adam Smith Institute.

6 THE IMPORTANCE OF ENTREPRENEURSHIP IN THE UK EXPRESS COACH MARKET

Graham Parkhurst[1]

Expectations of entrepreneurship

One of the more subtle arguments in favour of both deregulation and privatisation of bus and coach services was that the legislation would free up the managers of the industry to be more entrepreneurial, whether in terms of making incremental changes to existing services, or trying out entirely new kinds of service in new places.

Two key figures who have now entered the folklore of the story of deregulation are Harry Blundred, active in the first decade of UK deregulation, and Brian Souter, the most famous bus entrepreneur in modern times, and still a driving force today. Blundred is credited with pioneering the use of smaller buses, with the most famous example being his launch of the Devon General minibus fleet in Exeter in the early days of deregulation (Wolmar, 1998). Souter made his name even earlier, as a pioneer provider of deregulated coach services after 1980, seeking new markets through innovations such as much lower fares and overnight services, and introducing features such as on-board refreshments (Stewart, 2005).

---

1 Dr Parkhurst is Senior Lecturer in Transport Planning at University of the West of England, Bristol. He has conducted research on transport policy since 1991, including on a range of public transport issues.

This chapter examines three contemporary initiatives which are closely associated with these entrepreneurs. These include: the emergence of low-cost express coach services nationally; the introduction of a commercially operated, long-distance, demand-responsive taxibus route; and ongoing innovation in the Oxford–London express coach market. The first and second of these are recent innovations which will be briefly reviewed, while the longer-established Oxford–London service is subject to more detailed analysis.

Mega-network

Stagecoach Group's Megabus network is a logical development of Stagecoach's long-standing involvement in the express coach sector. New technology – the Internet – played a key facilitating role in creating the market niche for the network. Most passengers book in advance online, and yield management is used to ensure efficient vehicle loadings, thereby following the key principles in the success of the low-cost airlines. Fares are available on all routes from £1 per trip (plus a £0.50 booking fee).

Having operated trial routes from August 2003, the national network was unveiled in February 2004, and now serves 34 destinations using more than 60 vehicles, including 25 double-deck coaches, and is expected to achieve profitability during 2005/06. The product is aimed at generating new markets, and the availability of genuinely low fares to most travellers is seen as fundamental. While the target market was younger travellers, other less expected sources of patronage have emerged, including 'silver surfers'. Some routes are also used by commuters, who tend to book journeys for a week or more in one visit to the website (ibid.).

The inaugural route was between Oxford and London. This was a logical choice, despite this being the most frequently served express coach route in Europe, owing in part to the belief that Megabus would appeal to new markets, but also because the vehicles take advantage of existing Stagecoach depot facilities, and knowledge of the market obtained through operating the 'Oxford Tube' service on the route. Evidence that the network is serving a new market comes from the fact that National Express, the most established market player, has continued to see around 5 per cent annual passenger growth across its network, simultaneous with the expansion of the network and passenger base of Megabus (ibid.).

Although the Oxford–London route reached break-even in eight months (Whincup, 2004), it was subsequently transformed into what is probably the first 'virtual' bus route. The liveried vehicles themselves are now integrated into the Oxford Tube fleet and Megabus passengers in practice buy a discounted ticket in advance for a specific Tube departure. This further enhances the efficiency of the two operations, while extending discounting to all Tube departures. The same approach has also been applied to other routes, such as Stagecoach Express X5 (Cambridge–Oxford).

Two similar commercial initiatives by other organisations are notable. One was the launch of easyBus by Easy Group entrepreneur Stelios Haji-Ioannou on routes from London to Milton Keynes and Luton Airport; this also relies on yield management and Internet pre-booking. Although seen by some commentators (e.g. Whincup, 2004) as a competitive response to Megabus, these routes are low-capacity, served by a total of ten sixteen-seat mini-buses (Easy Group, 2005). Synergy with Easy Group's core low-cost airline activity from Luton Airport, and perhaps the presence of the easyCinema in Milton Keynes, may have been important factors in the selection of the two routes, in addition to the competitive impulse. The other response, from National Express, was the introduction of 'funfares', a more obvious competitive measure. These are limited allocations of low-cost, restricted tickets for advance purchase on the Internet. As with Megabus, fares start from £1.

Yellow Taxibus

A specific belief of the proponents of deregulation was that market niches existed for bus services to become much closer to their passengers, through the use of smaller vehicles – perhaps taxis operating as buses – running more flexibly in time and space. In practice, although services showed a greater tendency to penetrate residential estates following deregulation, in response to consumer demand (Wolmar, 1998), the nature of the operations has remained one of relatively large vehicles running on fixed routes and schedules.[2]

Although there were experiments with 'taxibus'-type services before and after 1985, including the Milton Keynes dial-a-ride network in the early 1970s and the current semi-commercial Bicester Taxibus,[3] it took until August 2003 for a convincing and radical experiment to emerge. Stagecoach's Yellow Taxibus linking

2 Ironically, part of the reason for this is that the legislation itself placed great emphasis on route registrations, with traffic commissioners empowered with sanctions to ensure that buses were *not* flexible, but stuck rigidly to routes and timetables.

3 Operated by a taxi firm from Bicester North station on behalf of Chiltern Trains, with vehicles leased from Oxfordshire County Council.

Dunfermline and Edinburgh is radical because it is an entirely private sector initiative, while most other contemporary demand-responsive services are very much public sector inspired. The nature of the operation is also significant: effectively an express coach service operated by eight-seat vehicles over a 30-kilometre route, and with peak headways as low as ten minutes. Individual fares for the shared vehicles are available from £4 single.

The service operates in demand-responsive mode with telephone booking from a specified area of Dunfermline, but uses conventional bus stops from the outskirts of Dunfermline into central Edinburgh. No special subsidies have been sought, but the fixed section of the route is eligible for an 80 per cent refund of fuel tax incurred under Bus Service Operators' Grant (BSOG) arrangements, and Fife Council concessionary fare card holders can travel at half-fare, but these are a small proportion of customers (Andrew, 2005).

Special success factors associated with the service include the identification of a new market: relatively wealthy Dunfermline–Edinburgh commuters whose modal alternative would be the car, as the locale is hard to serve with conventional buses, and taxis would be prohibitively expensive to use in most circumstances. Supporting transport policy factors include the existence of bus priorities from the Forth Road Bridge to the centre of Edinburgh, the Forth Bridge toll and high parking charges in Edinburgh. The willingness of the traffic commissioner to assist in negotiating a way through the regulatory framework was also significant – although even with a positive relationship this nonetheless took two years. Much effort has also been devoted to targeted marketing, with the focus on building a novel modal identity. Capital costs have been minimised by using relatively low-technology booking and dispatching arrangements, and running costs have been reduced by the use of vehicles that can be driven with a car licence.

Data in the public domain to date show steady patronage growth (Andrew, 2004), while Stagecoach expects to report on the service, including its financial performance, by the end of 2005. The experience has already been used to establish a feeder taxibus service connecting with the South West Trains network at Petersfield, and also to win tendered services in Aberdeen City, Aberdeenshire and Fife (Andrew, 2005).

Oxford–London: 'Tube' or 'Espress'?

The Oxford–London express coach market is a well-known deregulation success story which emerged after 1985. Long-establishment does not imply stasis, however, and the services offer interesting examples of recent innovation.

The potential to compete with the established City of Oxford Motor Services was spotted by Thames Transit's Harry Blundred soon after deregulation, with the 'Oxford Tube' branding – implying an extension to London's public transport network – proving an inspired choice. Competition in the market continues to exist between two coach operators, in addition to the 'substitute goods' of rail and car. Competition has promoted innovation as a means of maintaining market share and attracting new passengers. The two services have for many years operated on a 24-hour basis, with headways as low as ten to twelve minutes at peak times.

Recent innovation has included the purchase by Stagecoach Oxfordshire of a fleet of 81-seat double-deck vehicles for the

'Tube', which means that the company has around two-thirds of the capacity on the route (and in fact a similar share of the patronage). The Go-Ahead subsidiary Oxford Bus Company has also purchased high-specification single-deck vehicles and adopted a sharp marketing campaign for its Espress service, with the intention of creating a premium brand. The combined investment in the two modern vehicle fleets has been one of the largest in the UK bus sector on a specific route.

In practice, competition has not resulted in wide differentiation in the services offered: both companies use vehicles which are air-conditioned and are equipped with closed-circuit television for security, power points and toilets. The 45/46-seat single-deckers used on the Espress have particularly generous legroom in keeping with the branding policy, while the Tube vehicles have low-floor access. The service frequencies show very similar patterns, with minor differences relating to scheduling in the early hours of the morning, but with little consequence for the comparative number of departures. Both companies have completely flexible booking arrangements, including walk-on and advance purchase in person, by phone or by Internet. The range of tickets and fares is very closely aligned. The single and return prices are identical for full-price and concessionary tickets: only some multi-ride and season tickets have modest differences.

In addition to private sector entrepreneurship, part of the success of the route may be due to the public sector and market context: both Oxford and London have constrained environments for car travel, and for decades have had local transport policies that favoured bus for intra-city travel, with high resulting modal shares. Tangible factors such as relatively low car ownership, and less intangible ones, such as attitudes towards bus use, have no doubt assisted patronage development, as have the specific market demographics, which include 'easy win' groups such as students, tourists and public-transport-dependent commuters.

Go-Ahead group claims BSOG on the 5 kilometres of Espress route in Oxford and 25 kilometres of the route in London. A stop on the Oxford Tube was introduced on the M40 motorway at Lewknor (Junction 6) in Blundred's time, which attracts informal park-and-ride and kiss-and-ride patronage,[4] and Stagecoach can claim for the Oxford–Lewknor (20-kilometre) leg as a result as well.[5] BSOG in general terms can offset around 10 per cent of operating costs (Atkins, 2003). Sutton (2005) understood that subsidy may have played a part in justifying the introduction of the stop, but reports that it now has self-sustaining levels of patronage, and would not be withdrawn in the absence of BSOG. Similarly, Eggleton (2005) was confident that BSOG was not important enough to influence the Espress stopping pattern, with the Hillingdon stop, which results in the largest proportion of BSOG payment for the route, being itself revenue-generating. Eggleton also confirmed that the extension of the 50 per cent public subsidy for concessionary fares to express coach services also brought in useful additional revenue, but noted that the number of eligible passengers had not noticeably altered the market. On balance, subsidy has played a relatively small role in both services, particularly in recent years, and the most likely response to withdrawal would be to seek to increase load factors rather than increase ticket prices or reduce services (Sutton, 2005).

4 The stop recently benefited from being linked to a state-supported demand-responsive transport service.

5 This leg falls just inside the 15-mile inter-stop distance eligibility criterion for scheduled long-distance coach routes.

The alternative rail service is an obvious feature of the operating environment for express coaches to London, with the substitutable good being the limited-stop rail service on the alignment via Reading, running with a 30-minute headway during the day and timetabled to take around 55 minutes. Rail services are hence less frequent, and the route is somewhat indirect and congested, creating a level of unreliability, but rail travel is usually faster.

For this reason, comparative fares levels are an important consideration. In general, coach fares in the South-East of England are around 30 per cent lower than parallel rail journeys, this difference reflecting the greater travel time involved (Atkins, 2003). The coach fares Oxford–London for most off-peak day-return fares (09:00–15:00) are in fact 25 per cent cheaper. In the morning peak period, however, the coach saving is greater than 60 per cent, and after 15:00 greater than 50 per cent. The comparison is complicated by the fact that the coach tickets allow return the following day, which is not available with off-peak day-return rail fares, while the travel-time differential is more favourable to rail at peak times. Overall, the rail–coach comparisons support the view that certain groups of travellers in the Oxford–London market are particularly price sensitive, with implications for both demand and mode choice, and that the coach operators have been able to minimise a peaking in coach demand by exploiting the relatively inflexible rail tariff structures, which reflect national as well as local considerations.

While politics, geography and economics offer partial explanations, though, the importance of historical coincidence through the action of entrepreneurs remains important, as comparative consideration of the Cambridge–London express coach route seems to confirm.

Table 1 **Comparison of walk-on fares (August 2005)**

Route	*Coach – day return*	*Coach – overnight return*	*Rail – standard return*	*Rail – off-peak day return*
Oxford–London	£12.00*	£12.00	£32.50	£16.00
Cambridge–London	£9.80	£15.00	£26.00	£17.00

*A £7.00 return is available for departures from 1500.

Cambridge has a roughly similar population to Oxford, is located a similar distance via motorway from London, and has comparable settlement form and functions to Oxford, including a travel market with important student and tourist shares. The sole operator of express coach services to London (National Express), however, offers just sixteen direct departures over an eighteen-hour operating day. Journey times to the first central London stop are similar to those from Oxford.[6] Given the importance of Stagecoach in the Cambridge bus market, and the similarities with Oxford, a question is raised as to why there is no 'Cambridge Tube'.

Oxford–London and Cambridge–London rail services are roughly comparable: both offer direct, express services. Off-peak tickets are slightly more expensive from Cambridge; peak tickets rather more expensive from Oxford (Table 1). Day-return coach travel from Cambridge is 20 per cent cheaper than from Oxford (although Oxford coach passengers can in fact return the next day with this fare).

Norwell (2005) reports that the combined capacity of National Express coach services and the rail services caters for expressed

6 The Cambridge service takes longer to reach the Victoria Coach Station terminus given that this is on the south-western side of central London.

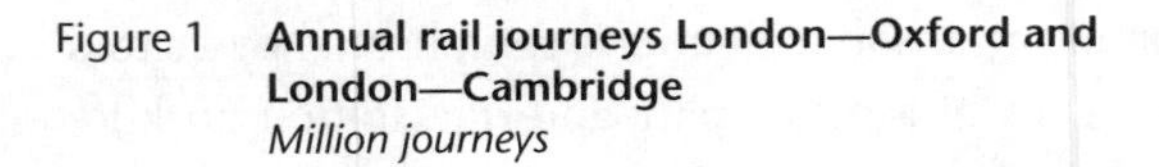

Figure 1 **Annual rail journeys London—Oxford and London—Cambridge**
Million journeys

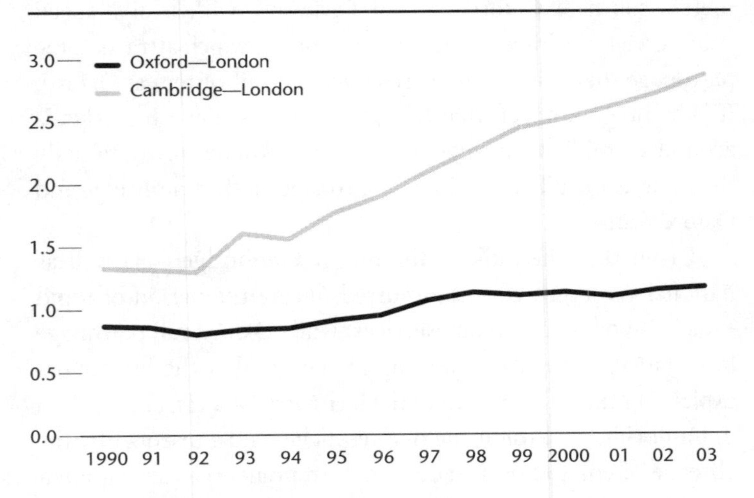

Source: Data kindly provided by D. Greeno, Statistics Team, Office of Rail Regulation

demand, but acknowledges that the Oxford and Cambridge comparison is a striking one and that there may be potential for the Cambridge–London market to develop. He notes historical changes in ownership as being possibly relevant explanatory factors for why this has not occurred to date, with Cambridge Coach Services – and Stagecoach itself – having been earlier operators on the route.

In this context it is notable that the number of rail journeys to and from London and Cambridge has more than doubled in the last fifteen years, while much more modest growth has occurred London–Oxford (Figure 1).

Comparison of the absolute figures is complicated by factors such as the existence of a major park-and-ride station 20 kilometres south of Oxford (Didcot Parkway), with a high-speed train service reaching London in 40 minutes, which attracts some patronage that would otherwise access the rail system at Oxford. It is notable, however, that the Oxford–London coach market is around 2.5 million passengers per annum (Atkins, 2003), broadly the same as the difference in rail patronage on the Cambridge and Oxford routes.

Given that the bulk of the recent Cambridge – as well as national – rail growth has occurred during the period of rapid expansion of Oxford coach services, while Oxford rail patronage has changed little, it is tempting to suggest that the key factors explaining the difference were the lack, first, of a Harry Blundred in Cambridge to exploit the market niche, and subsequently the absence of competition leading to entrepreneurial development and adaptation of the services, as in Oxford.

Conclusions

Each of the case studies exhibits contextual factors that may not be reproducible in other localities, such as specific traveller markets, and 'bus-friendly' local transport policies. They also share factors that can be reproduced, however, such as effective marketing, and working in innovative ways within the existing regulatory and fiscal frameworks, including taking advantage of subsidies to assist with pump-priming (but then developing the business so it is not dependent on them). Support is also found for the principle that developing mutually supportive innovative services can be particularly effective, with a tentative indication that demand-

Whincup, T. (2004), 'EasyGroup jumpstarts no-frills bus', CNN International News, 29 April, <http://edition.cnn.com/2004/TRAVEL/04/29/easybus/index.html> (accessed 3 August).

Wolmar, C. (1998), *Stagecoach: A Classic Rags-to-Riches Tale from the Frontiers of Capitalism*, London: Orion Business Books.

7 RUNNING FREE – PRIVATE OWNERSHIP OF ROADS

Oliver Knipping[1]

Unexpected allies

Road pricing has become fashionable in recent years. While this development may be surprising only at first glance, it was partly helped by statists, primarily pursuing different goals from those of champions of the free market. Whether the statists' U-turn is due to an epiphany, or to more understandable communication from the advocates of free market policies, the road is leading towards pricing.

There are several objectives of road pricing from a liberal economist's perspective. It can be used to internalise external costs caused by congestion and imposed on the environment; to help establish proper transport planning and traffic management by using the price mechanism and information contained in price signals; and to provide safe and high-quality road space for consumers by ensuring that infrastructure is built in response to road users' preferences rather than bureaucrats' preferences.

Rather more appealing to the socialist mindset is road pricing as a restraint measure,[2] or one of environmental or budgetary

1 Oliver Knipping, PhD, president, Institute for Free Enterprise, Berlin, www.unternehmerische-freiheit.de. The author dedicates this contribution to the loving memory of his father, who died on 22 June 2005.

2 Roth (1998: 13) concludes that, if congestion charges are used as envisaged in the 1997 Road Traffic Reduction Act, 'as a "highly effective restraint measure",

relief. Whereas environmental objectives are an implicit goal of the internalisation of external costs and fully in compliance with market economics,[3] pre-determined traffic reductions irrespective of users' preferences and the use of revenues as additional taxation to further redistribute income are major objectives in the mindset of those statists who support road pricing. Notwithstanding their objectives, though, the outcome has been an increase in toll roads and a move towards the public acceptance of pricing.

Roads for sale

The public debate is centred on pricing of roads, leaving the ownership question untouched. Is the limitation to road user charging based on economic rationale, pragmatism or the culture of compromise with statists? Prerequisites for both pricing and commercialisation of road infrastructure are engineering, economic and political in nature (Day, 1998: 5)

Road pricing is now technically feasible.[4] Engineering difficulties preventing road pricing have been resolved by technologies such as GPS and UMTS.[5] Vehicles equipped with an on-board

congestion pricing could become an instrument of tyranny enabling governments to increase their powers by extracting rents from the use of monopolised infrastructure'. The Department for Transport, Local Government and the Regions (1998) embarks on the same mission.

3 Day (1998: 5) reminds us that environmentalism is an inherent concept of the free market: 'Since long before environmentalism was even heard of, economists have argued that social costs … include the adverse impact on others of pollution and other externalities. … For many decades, economists have argued that the polluter should pay.'

4 Hills (1998: 31); see Blythe (2004: 361–4) and Blythe and Pickford (2004) for a comprehensive overview of technical charging options.

5 See Birle (2004) for application of both GSM and 3G technologies for electronic fee collection.

charging unit may provide individual customers with intelligent traffic management that may calculate road charges prior to the trip according to applicable prices during specific times of day, routes selected and congestion charges at the time of travel. Additionally, such a system may also provide alternative choices to users, ranking route options by costs, travel duration and road congestion. An intelligent traffic management system would considerably stimulate competition between different roads.

The recently implemented German toll collection scheme is based on GPS technology, embracing automatic toll collection via an on-board unit, but is currently restricted to trucks over 12 tonnes on all German motorways. The technology locates vehicles with a precision of around 10 metres and automatically monitors compliance via installed sensors on 300 bridges and additionally staffed mobile enforcement units.[6] However advanced, this charging technology is still in an early stage of innovation.

At the heart of the slow political uptake lies the perceived public good character of road networks. Further analysis of the two underlying principles of public goods, non-exclusivity and non-rivalry for products (Blankart, 2003: 57), however, shows that road infrastructure exhibits the typical characteristics of private rather than public goods. Various forms of tolling and payment schemes including penalties for non-compliance prove that road users are excludable from roads. It is clear that major roads and urban roads, at least, do not exhibit non-rivalry. Road space is scarce and road users compete for it.

Nevertheless, road infrastructure has characteristics that are commonly assigned to so-called public goods, such as positive

6 www.toll-collect.de; see Kossak (2004) for a brief summary.

and negative externalities regarding the investment climate and its impact on the economy, as well as environmental and other damage that has so far not been borne by their producers. These externalities, however, may be internalised by an efficient system of road pricing.

The theory of public goods is closely related to both economic and political reservations regarding private road provision and operation. Notwithstanding the principles of exclusivity and rivalry characterising road infrastructure as private goods, economics does not necessarily have an impact on public perception. This is even more so as it was convenient for politicians to sell road infrastructure developments as 'public projects' and thus keep them in the sphere of influence of politicians. As public choice theory revealed, politicians are not driven by altruistic motivations, but by their desire for re-election and the maximisation of their own utility functions. Privatisation of road assets considerably reduces politicians' realm of influence over transport policy. Road pricing itself has been sold by politicians, not on economic grounds but on the grounds of environmental concerns and budgetary relief linked to redistribution of income. This is an approach that keeps politicians in control both of the revenue and of road assets. Less than limited enthusiasm may be expected for private road provision and operation combined with road pricing. The initial focus on pricing is thus a pragmatic compromise due to political constraints. The use of a complex tax system, overcharging for road use and the redistribution of road user charges to other government projects are the major impediments to applying economic rationale to road policy.

Economically efficient road prices should be combined with the elimination of vehicle licensing fees and of fuel taxes that are largely independent of actual road usage and the scarcity of road space used. Efficient prices cannot be designed by well-meaning economists, planners or politicians whether they believe in a state-controlled or in a free market economy. Efficient prices are the outcome of a competitive marketplace where a myriad of decisions based on dispersed knowledge are coordinated. This was Hayek's strong message during his Nobel Prize Lecture:

> It is indeed the source of the superiority of the market order ... that in the resulting allocation of resources more of the knowledge of particular facts will be utilized which exists only dispersed among uncounted persons, than any one person can possess. But because we, the observing scientists, can thus never know all the determinants of such an order, and in consequence also cannot know at which particular structure of prices and wages demand would everywhere equal supply, we also cannot measure the deviations from that order ... (from Hayek, 1992)

He concludes: 'a communications system which we call the market ... turns out to be a more efficient mechanism for digesting dispersed information than any that man has deliberately designed' (ibid.).

Notwithstanding concerns about political feasibility, implementing an efficient pricing system under state ownership is a contradiction in terms as it cripples market pricing and its essential allocation and signalling functions and replaces it with centrally administered command pricing according to political considerations, such as those previously mentioned. As observed by Mises, efficiency may not be the primary objective of bureaucrats, as

> ... authorities are inclined to deviate from the profit system. ... They consider the accomplishment of other tasks more important ... Whatever these other goals aimed at may be, the result of such a policy always amounts to subsidizing some people to the burden of others ... If ... a city-owned transportation system charges the customers so low a fare that the costs of the operation cannot be covered, the taxpayers are virtually subsidizing those riding the trains. (Mises, 1996: 62–3)

Free the roads – towards a market for road infrastructure

Though the idea of efficiency itself may be broadly welcome, the term is open to broad interpretations adapted to individual liking rather than necessarily being related to the outcome of undistorted competitive supply and demand. Private ownership is likely to be refuted instantly by arguing that road infrastructure is monopolistic in its structure.

Indeed, today's road infrastructure is run as a monopoly under public ownership. But then it is rather Kafkaesque to assume that this means that the monopolistic structure is necessarily a feature of road provision when, in fact, market provision and operation has deliberately been excluded and crowded out by state ownership. As public supply of existing infrastructure does not necessarily reflect customers' demand, the system would be potentially inefficient if it were simply to be sold to private investors. This mismatch, however, is by no means a market failure, but must be assigned to the current, government, owners of the existing road network and not to private operators.

Private ownership of road networks implies both privatisation of existing roads and private provision of potential additional road space. Irrespective of political considerations, the first step towards the development of private road operations is also the most difficult one.[7] Devising stretches of roads or networks to be sold to private operators must not anticipate any market structure, adding to already existent imperfections of a public monopoly. As a solution, comparatively small units may be auctioned off to private investors, who may at the same time tender for as many lots as they wish without any restriction on merging or selling their property after the initial road purchase. The second step is concerned with road investment or disinvestment subject to supply and demand signals, to be undertaken by the incumbents or entrants to the road market.

Rather than implementing road pricing prior to the commercialisation of roads, the infrastructure should be sold outright. The eventual pricing decisions would then be left to individual road operators, subject to the use of charges to facilitate the internalisation of environmental externalities. Businesses owning roads should not be allowed to apply for public subsidy or political favours of any kind, and this approach should apply to the entire network, from highways to local roads, from inter-urban roads to metropolitan road infrastructure. As a counterpart to internalisation of external costs for private road operators, the state should retreat from meddling with the road industry, whether regarding regulations in the name of a presupposed public interest or

7 Roth (1998: 10) considers that 'large-scale privatisation of existing roads is not yet a viable option. A market solution would encourage the private provision of new road links, but the privatisation of existing roads would be much more difficult. As roads are not now run on a commercial basis, their earning power is unknown, and there is no financial basis for setting privatisation prices'. He concludes that roads should be commercialised prior to privatisation.

the imposition of vehicle licensing fees and fuel taxes to raise revenues.

As the road operators would determine their own charging structure, we may only guess how an efficient pricing system could develop in a competitive road and transport network. Owing to the wide availability of GPS and UMTS networks, these technologies may be applied to provide the charging technology, rather than using tolling booths or number-plate recognition. Some operators applying prices to enter a particular zone, rather than using point-to-point charging, such as those in conurbations, may use number-plate recognition. This approach is used in the London charging zone today (Transport for London, 2005). Also, some operators may prefer to use tolling booths, for example, along motorways. New charging technologies will, of course, be discovered. Operators may develop a common charging standard, for example via use of GPS technology, to ease the handling of payments, increase traffic flow and make their charges and offers transparent to users of intelligent on-board traffic management units.

With regard to the process of internalising external costs, road operators are likely to pass the costs on to road users and charge the marginal social costs for road use. Though road operators are most likely to charge users directly, they may also retreat to more unconventional methods, such as indirect charging by selling advertising space along the road or on on-board units, as long as this does not interfere with road safety and security.

Road pricing and the efficiency of the transport industry: the link to Hibbs

Road user pricing will have an impact on the entire transport industry, as '… the object of the exercise is to enable road users to make rational decisions, and so to improve the efficiency of the market for movement'.[8] Pricing is likely to have some effect on the modal shift, depending on the competitive response in other transport industries. Glaister and Graham imply direct benefits for bus and taxi users due to increased speeds and greater reliability.[9] Whereas this holds true for urban traffic, as evident in the London charging scheme (Transport for London, 2005), it similarly applies to highway traffic. Reduced congestion would 'enable the express coach industry to perform far more efficiently, promoting innovation and growth, in healthy competition with both the car and the train'.[10]

Freeing the roads from the realm of political meddling by means of private ownership leads to an efficient transport infrastructure that internalises external costs and reflects the individual preferences of road users. Statists have long acted as beholders of a proclaimed public interest. It is time for customers to take over. Hibbs understood the need for a competitive bus industry, free from political interference. Hibbs also understood that the bus industry could benefit from an environment in which

8 Hibbs (2003b: 86); see Knipping (2002) on a market for railways in the absence of government intervention.

9 Glaister and Graham (2004: 38–46); the authors also draw on the latest results from the London congestion charging scheme.

10 Hibbs and Bradley (1997: 37); see also Hibbs (1998: 3). Hibbs (2003a: 21) notes bus managers predicting that they could operate more reliable services, attract more passengers and save some 20 per cent of both capital and operating costs if congestion were avoided.

all road users paid the marginal costs of their journeys and that the combination of a competitive bus industry and road pricing was necessary to reap the full benefits of a market economy. The private ownership and provision of roads is also necessary, though. The infrastructure on which the various transport modes run should be provided in a competitive environment and priced through a process that is free from political interference. All these policies are self-reinforcing. The private provision of roads would remove the perceived need for politicians to interfere in the allocation of road space, through traffic management schemes and the like.[11] Pricing of roads would remove the perceived need for politicians to interfere in the market to provide special favours (such as subsidies) to the bus and rail industry, special favours that are invariably accompanied by political interference.

References

Birle, C. (2004), 'Use of GSM and 3G cellular radio for electronic fee collection', IEE seminar on Road User Charging, London, 9 June, www.iee.org.

Blankart, C. B. (2003), *Öffentliche Finanzen in der Demokratie*, Munich: Verlag Vahlen.

Blythe, P. T. (2004), 'Congestion charging: challenges to meet the UK policy objectives', *Review of Network Economics*, 3(4): 356–70.

11 Although private owners of roads will develop their own mechanisms of allocating road space so that available space is allocated efficiently, taking into account the needs of all users.

Blythe, P. T. and A. Pickford (2004), 'Road user charging in the UK: where will we be in 2014?', IEE seminar on Road User Charging, London, 9 June, www.iee.org.

Day, A. (1998), 'The case for road pricing', *IEA Economic Affairs*, 18(4): 5–8.

Department for Transport, Local Government and the Regions (1998), *A New Deal for Transport: Better for Everyone*, White Paper, London: HMSO.

Glaister, S. and D. J. Graham (2004), *Pricing Our Roads: Vision and Reality*, London: Institute for Economic Affairs.

Hayek, F. A. (1992), 'The pretence of knowledge', in A. Lindbeck (ed.), *Nobel Lectures, Economics 1969–1980*, Singapore: World Scientific Publishing, www.nobelprize.org.

Hibbs, J. (1998), 'Editorial: a radical approach', *IEA Economic Affairs*, 18(4): 2–4.

Hibbs, J. (2003a), *Running Buses: Who knows best what passengers want?*, London: Adam Smith Institute.

Hibbs, J. (2003b), *Transport Economics and Policy*, London: Kogan Page.

Hibbs, J. and M. Bradley (1997), *Deregulated Decade. Ten Years of Bus Deregulation*, London: Adam Smith Institute.

Hills, P. (1998), 'Implementing road-use pricing by stealth', *IEA Economic Affairs*, 18(4): 31–6.

Knipping, O. (2002), *The Liberalisation of European Railway Markets – Laissez-faire versus Interventionism*, PhD thesis, University College London.

Kossak, A. (2004), 'Tolling Heavy Goods Vehicles on Germany's autobahns', IEE seminar on Road User Charging, London, 9 June, www.iee.org.

Mises, L. V. (1996), *Bureaucracy*, Grove City: Libertarian Press, www.mises.org.

Roth, G. (1998), 'Road pricing in a free society', *IEA Economic Affairs*, 18(4): 9–14.

Transport for London (2005), *Central London Congestion Charging Scheme Impacts Monitoring Summary Review: January 2005*, www.tfl.gov.uk.

8 MARKETING AWARENESS IN THE BUS INDUSTRY: THREATS TO PROGRESS

Paul Kevill[1]

Why worry about marketing?

The threat to business freedom from the re-regulation of the bus industry is serious enough, yet we face the loss of something just as fundamental – its companion tool, the marketing mix. The contribution of Professor John Hibbs to the intellectual basis for the 1985 Transport Act is rightly recognised, but his contribution went far beyond the theoretical ideas. I am indebted to him, as are many of his former students, for a grounding in the practical application of marketing principles to transport. Despite the industry's common excuses (for instance, that 'you can't sell buses like baked beans'), he has shown how the original 'Four Ps' of marketing (Product, Price, Place and Promotion) map well on to bus services (Hibbs, 1989).

It is a grounding that perhaps all transport practitioners should have, whether they are in the public or the private sector. Without it, we find that even at the highest levels of government and among respected writers, 'marketing' is simply equated with promotion and publicity and is almost always treated as an add-on, or something that happens as a 'campaign'. This is more than just semantics – at best it invites planners to ignore the rest of the

1 Freelance consultant and researcher and visiting lecturer in transport planning at Sheffield Hallam University. Formerly business analyst at South Yorkshire PTE.

marketing mix. At worst it might prompt a puritanical rejection of the whole concept as pushy, invasive sales trickery instead of being a complete basis for customer-oriented business.

Despite the opportunities inherent in the 1985 act for marketing to emerge as a tool and a business orientation, the production orientation that was generally held to characterise public sector provision persisted among many private bus businesses. Experience from other sectors of post-privatisation behaviour suggested lengthy periods (say five, ten or even fifteen years) for a cultural shift to occur, and among bus companies it seemed particularly slow and patchy.

My research into this phenomenon, supervised by Professor Hibbs and building on his previous work (Hibbs, 1991a), suggested that managers with a customer orientation had always been there, distributed randomly among the former National Bus Company, Passenger Transport Executives, municipals and independents, but had been working within a system that stifled innovation. We have seen how some of them have flourished once the restrictions were removed, but continuing regulation and public sector intervention were found to have been contributing factors that limited the development of marketing mixes.

Progress has been made in marketing, but an indication of how stubborn product orientation has been is that 'placing the customer first' is still news in the transport press, and 'making your problem the customer's problem' is still too common.

Yet even before the benefits of a marketing orientation have been fully exploited, the freedom to do so is under threat. The new danger to enterprise is that bus operators become contractors, in the style of refuse collectors, distanced from their consumers.

Shots in the foot and banana skins

In mounting a defence of private enterprise in bus services, we can again call on John Hibbs's intellectual foundations of deregulation. There are three of his ideas that seem particularly relevant at present:

- his comparison of the risk-taking behaviour of the public and private sectors with implications for contestability in the market;
- the nature of marketing and the centrality of *people* to it;
- liberalisation as an 'uncompleted enterprise' in which road pricing needs to feature.

They can be used to demonstrate how the public sector has provided 'banana skins' for the industry to slip on, but they might also present the private sector with challenges where the theory has been let down by the delivery through complacency and the industry 'shooting itself in the foot'.

Risk and returns

A favourite illustration of Hibbs is a paraphrase of Dr Johnson: 'Depend upon it, Sir, that when a man knows he is to go out of business, it concentrates the mind wonderfully.'

This serves to remind us of the fundamental difference between enterprise in pursuit of profit and subsidy management. In the former, the imperative is to serve customers, and they judge success by – as Baker (1991) puts it – 'casting their money votes daily'. In a profit-making organisation, the more customers are served, the healthier the business and the more customers are attracted.

In public sector delivery based on subsidy, the more people are served, the more it costs. There is little incentive to expand or innovate, and budgetary pressures and fear of political embarrassment give an incentive not to serve people *too* well.

To create new business for survival and growth one must take risks – this is central to any preference for private enterprise over public provision. Yet re-regulators are able to seize (selectively) on the private sector's apparently routine, cost-plus fare increases, retrenchment and consistently poor service as evidence of private sector aversion to risk, and of contestability being merely theoretical. A strong tendency towards territoriality also gives local authorities the impression that bus operators do not really fear competition.

In addition, the local authority (LA) subsidy culture might be said to have sucked in bus companies to some extent. One of the most notable post-1986 shots in the foot was customer information, inviting LA intervention. That operators are willing to rely on potential customers receiving sales information second hand is a 'serious criticism of the marketing management of the bus industry' (Hibbs, 1993).

Another banana skin (left by the 1985 act) was that the LAs were able to take some 40 per cent of the industry's customers for themselves, with concessionary fares preventing the private sector from competing on price for important segments. Free travel for pensioners turns the operator into a subcontractor, with the potential for re-regulation of a sort, by the back door, with surprisingly little opposition.

Paradoxically, though, it might be that the insulated state of bureaucrats permits them to take risks, whilst the turnover-based profit targets (or even precarious state) of private bus operators caution against it. The low political profile of transport and lack of measurable targets or real accountability mean that heads roll far less frequently in the public sector if it fails to deliver.

Sometimes the public sector's role in underwriting risk is even made explicit. In Stagecoach's 'Kickstart' proposal – pump-priming for bus routes with uncertain prospects – local authorities are invited to provide subsidy while patronage builds up to profitable levels. Recently, *Transit* (2005) reported that Stagecoach pursued some such routes anyway, with success, when they failed to attract such funding.

So it comes about that re-regulators can convince themselves that the entrepreneurial spark is not all it is said to be, but that they can use the private sector to handle the painful business of cost-cutting.

The risks the best of the bus operators have taken have been as much about the way they do things, not just in the popular media image of risk as massive capital investment. Taking risks with *people* and *process* is something we must look to the private sector for, which brings us to another of Professor Hibbs's most notable contributions.

Service comes from people, not structures

Marketing of services is often treated differently from the marketing of tangible products, although in a sense all business is a service because consumers choose a 'meaningful bundle of rational and emotive benefits' (Salama, 1994), of which physical goods are only a part. From a busman's perspective, John Hibbs has stressed the importance to this of *people* and *process* in delivering both rational and emotive parts of travel.

These 'fifth and sixth Ps' of the marketing mix are important because the consumer has to be involved in the delivery so it matters *how* the service is delivered, and in a service industry where the company's product is in the hands of remote and largely unsupervised staff, those people are crucial to success.

We can observe, however, that the public sector and opponents of a competitive system tend to focus on 'structures' and 'frameworks', as if a successful outcome were merely the consequence of their proper design. This commodity-like view of bus services, bought by the hour or the mile, ignores the fact that structures deliver nothing; only people can deliver.

With its roots in the highly deterministic disciplines of civil engineering and traffic management, computer modelling of networks heavily influences decisions in public sector transport planning. Planners expect to be able to deconstruct observed behaviour into elasticities of demand that can theoretically predict travellers' responses to changes. Yet modelling tends to focus on the most easily modelled variables and not necessarily those most important to the customer or, more crucially, the potential customer.

A marketing/behavioural approach recognises consumers' rational and emotive choices, whereas in a transport planning approach consumers are self-optimising robots, concerned only with time or ('generalised') cost savings. Delighting the customer is replaced by 'meeting the needs' of 'users' (in language redolent of recipients of charity or people with a heroin habit).

As with risk-taking, however, the reality is that the private sector has not always performed true to type, and neither has the public sector. In a sense, bus operators have their own rationalists, in the shape of accountants, and the *people* part of the mix may have suffered as result. In the less customer-focused parts of the industry, hardware (such as vehicles, communications, point-of-sale electronics, guidance systems, etc.) has commanded greater attention than the 'soft' details of delivery. The latter can make or break customer satisfaction but is difficult to cost or allocate revenue to.

Meanwhile, the public sector is not without its consumer champions, and the Labour government has been quietly stealing the private sector's clothes. It responded to some extent to unfavourable comparisons of town hall bureaucracy with the private sector's approach to customers through the 'Best Value' process, in which a consumer-oriented approach (modified for the social service context) can be seen (DTLR, 1999). Perhaps predictably this promising approach to modernisation has run into bureaucracy and box-ticking, yet marketing-aware public sector managers will no longer be relying on the old 'we know best' philosophy. They will be making use of consumer research, and battles over whether the private sector is delivering could well be fought over whether the consumer is being well served. This ought to be the private sector's home ground, because a customer orientation is something they have that the public sector conventionally lacks. Yet the public sector is catching on, and is gathering feedback – sometimes unflattering – on what the private sector's customers think.

While marketing principles can be mapped on to bus services, however, there is very little room for manoeuvre in the important element of pricing. The nature of the 'uncompleted enterprise' means there are few opportunities for segmentation, particularly at the top end, which leads us to perhaps the greatest banana skin that the public sector has left us.

The 'uncompleted enterprise'

As we need to be continually reminded, 'deregulation' in the 1985 Transport Act was a misnomer. Many regulations remained, new ones were imposed and local authorities retained considerable powers of intervention. An analysis of transport, travel and land use might have identified market failure in the allocation of space, but it was not something that the government of the time was inclined to correct.

So it was that opening the bus industry to market forces failed to deal with the fundamentals of the total market for travel and persisted with subsidy as a 'second best' solution, hence the 'uncomplete enterprise' (Hibbs, 1991b).

This brings us to a more fundamental issue than either ownership or regulation. Consider the original mass transit marketing offer: large numbers of people want to go from A to B, and if they travel together, we can exploit efficiencies in fuel, vehicles and road space and this would be reflected in an attractive price for a professional (as opposed to 'DIY'[2]) transport service. Over time, changes in vehicle and fuel costs and licence-holding have eroded these advantages; the DIY version has become greatly superior to the 'professionally delivered' one.

The only Unique Selling Point that public transport then has left is its efficient use of land, particularly road space, but this has no market value. It relies heavily on unattractive and dying market segments. The problem is that such space is unpriced and simple microeconomics seems to offer an attractive explanation of the consequences: if the marginal price of consumption is zero, then it is consumed until its marginal utility is zero, i.e. it is 'wasted'.

2 In other words, driving.

We might observe that the same applies (despite fuel protests) to fuel consumption. In this context the waste in the 200-yard trip to the newsagent is an economic rather than a moral concept. There should be no need to talk about what journeys people should, or shouldn't, make by car, in the language of the planned economy; people are just using their 'money votes' according to their perception of the price/value trade off. Almost monthly, operators are reported to be trialling alternative-energy or energy-saving vehicle technology. Often the operators struggle with these experimental vehicles and their fuels. Again, although it might be good public relations, the theoretically valuable attribute of reducing emissions has no power in the market.

Worse still, it is not just a matter of the bus service being out-competed by car by reason of superiority, but that local authorities permit car traffic to corrupt the bus service offer. Congestion has the effect of a waste product that users dispose of for free by passing it on to other users, and this falls disproportionately on the bus service. This is contamination, as if Vodafone were allowed to drown out Orange's signals, or Tesco could cut their costs by dumping their empty boxes in Sainsbury's aisles. So the zero marginal cost of car use does not just waste resources because it makes a true price–quality comparison impossible, it actually *prevents* competitive marketing mixes from emerging.

Paying the full cost, levelling the playing field, internalising externalities, 'polluter pays', etc., are all fashionable terms. Congestion and pollution are said to need solutions urgently, and better public transport, particularly buses, is meant to be the answer. Yet local authorities wring their hands over the bus service attribute over which they have most influence, and the one consumers say is the most important – reliability. Regardless of ownership, what buses need is the 'level playing field' on the road. If local authorities cannot or will not sign up to this, arguably they shouldn't be telling operators how to operate, much less seeking to usurp their businesses.

Conclusions

The foregoing is intended to explore how we might continue to use Professor John Hibbs's ideas to refute arguments for re-regulation. The intellectual basis seems as sound as ever, and the decisive argument ought to be that the public sector has severely limited the scope for marketing innovation.

Proponents of re-regulation, however, are using arguments based on delivery and the private sector's behaviour (or at least caricatures of it). The challenge suggested by comparison of deregulation's promise and the current reality is that some bus operators have been inviting further intervention.

From instances of territoriality and risk aversion, local authorities have got the message that the threat of a quality contract has greater effect than a desire to win customers or the threat of competition. From examples of lack of customer focus among bus operators, local authorities get the idea that they might perform as well as private operators, and the greatest threat to enterprise is where a conservative or complacent bus company meets a marketing-aware local authority.

Some of the threat might be headed off through a rethink of 'cross-subsidy' in the context of the marketing paradigm as opposed to the blunt social instrument of the 1970s. Some companies already recognise that the whole offer, their network or their brand, is more important than how many pence you pay on any one journey.

Another option might be to pursue 'franchise' but in the more conventional sense of one private sector organisation delivering under the brand umbrella or systems of another. Bringing the private sector's best to a wider public in this way would doubtless be difficult for the big groups to swallow, but they are drawing most of the re-regulators' fire.

But even the best product is poisoned by congestion, although governments may be starting to see that public transport subsidy simply papers over the cracks in the market for total travel. It would be tragic if, within sight of a proper road pricing mechanism, the means to exploit it were taken away from bus companies.

References

Baker, M. J. (1991), 'One more time – what is marketing?', in M. J. Baker (ed.), *The Marketing Book*, Oxford: Butterworth-Heinemann, 2nd edn.

DTLR (Department for Transport, Local Government and the Regions) (1999), *Circular 10/99: Local Government Act 1999: Part I – Best Value*.

Hibbs, J. (1989), *Marketing Management in the Bus and Coach Industry*, Kingston upon Thames: Croner.

Hibbs, J. (1991a), 'An evaluation of urban bus deregulation in Britain: a survey of management attitudes', *Progress in Planning*, 36(3).

Hibbs, J. (1991b), 'The liberalisation of the British bus and coach industry: an uncompleted enterprise', *Economic Notes*, 38

Hibbs, J. (1993), *The Operation of Local Bus Services outside London: A response to the consultation paper issued by the Department of Transport*, June.

Kevill, P. (2003), *The Implications of Bus Operator Paradigms for Local Authority Intervention in Transport Markets*, Unpublished PhD thesis, University of Central England.

Salama, E. (1994), 'Hard-up punters throw a gloomy pall over the UK', *Marketing*, 24 March, p. 8.

Transit (2005), 'Celebrating "commercial Kickstart" success too loudly could alert the purse holders', 8 April, p. 23.

ABOUT THE IEA

The Institute is a research and educational charity (No. CC 235 351), limited by guarantee. Its mission is to improve understanding of the fundamental institutions of a free society with particular reference to the role of markets in solving economic and social problems.

The IEA achieves its mission by:

- a high-quality publishing programme
- conferences, seminars, lectures and other events
- outreach to school and college students
- brokering media introductions and appearances

The IEA, which was established in 1955 by the late Sir Antony Fisher, is an educational charity, not a political organisation. It is independent of any political party or group and does not carry on activities intended to affect support for any political party or candidate in any election or referendum, or at any other time. It is financed by sales of publications, conference fees and voluntary donations.

In addition to its main series of publications the IEA also publishes a quarterly journal, *Economic Affairs*.

The IEA is aided in its work by a distinguished international Academic Advisory Council and an eminent panel of Honorary Fellows. Together with other academics, they review prospective IEA publications, their comments being passed on anonymously to authors. All IEA papers are therefore subject to the same rigorous independent refereeing process as used by leading academic journals.

IEA publications enjoy widespread classroom use and course adoptions in schools and universities. They are also sold throughout the world and often translated/reprinted.

Since 1974 the IEA has helped to create a world-wide network of 100 similar institutions in over 70 countries. They are all independent but share the IEA's mission.

Views expressed in the IEA's publications are those of the authors, not those of the Institute (which has no corporate view), its Managing Trustees, Academic Advisory Council members or senior staff.

Members of the Institute's Academic Advisory Council, Honorary Fellows, Trustees and Staff are listed on the following page.

The Institute gratefully acknowledges financial support for its publications programme and other work from a generous benefaction by the late Alec and Beryl Warren.

iea

The Institute of Economic Affairs
2 Lord North Street, Westminster, London SW1P 3LB
Tel: 020 7799 8900
Fax: 020 7799 2137
Email: iea@iea.org.uk
Internet: iea.org.uk

Other papers recently published by the IEA include:

WHO, What and Why?

Transnational Government, Legitimacy and the World Health Organization

Roger Scruton

Occasional Paper 113; ISBN 0 255 36487 3

£8.00

The World Turned Rightside Up

A New Trading Agenda for the Age of Globalisation

John C. Hulsman

Occasional Paper 114; ISBN 0 255 36495 4

£8.00

The Representation of Business in English Literature

Introduced and edited by Arthur Pollard

Readings 53; ISBN 0 255 36491 1

£12.00

Anti-Liberalism 2000

The Rise of New Millennium Collectivism

David Henderson

Occasional Paper 115; ISBN 0 255 36497 0

£7.50

Capitalism, Morality and Markets

Brian Griffiths, Robert A. Sirico, Norman Barry & Frank Field

Readings 54; ISBN 0 255 36496 2

£7.50

A Conversation with Harris and Seldon

Ralph Harris & Arthur Seldon

Occasional Paper 116; ISBN 0 255 36498 9

£7.50

Malaria and the DDT Story

Richard Tren & Roger Bate

Occasional Paper 117; ISBN 0 255 36499 7

£10.00

A Plea to Economists Who Favour Liberty: Assist the Everyman

Daniel B. Klein

Occasional Paper 118; ISBN 0 255 36501 2

£10.00

The Changing Fortunes of Economic Liberalism

Yesterday, Today and Tomorrow

David Henderson

Occasional Paper 105 (new edition); ISBN 0 255 36520 9

£12.50

The Global Education Industry

Lessons from Private Education in Developing Countries

James Tooley

Hobart Paper 141 (new edition); ISBN 0 255 36503 9

£12.50

Saving Our Streams

The Role of the Anglers' Conservation Association in Protecting English and Welsh Rivers

Roger Bate

Research Monograph 53; ISBN 0 255 36494 6

£10.00

Better Off Out?

The Benefits or Costs of EU Membership

Brian Hindley & Martin Howe

Occasional Paper 99 (new edition); ISBN 0 255 36502 0

£10.00

Buckingham at 25

Freeing the Universities from State Control

Edited by James Tooley

Readings 55; ISBN 0 255 36512 8

£15.00

Lectures on Regulatory and Competition Policy

Irwin M. Stelzer

Occasional Paper 120; ISBN 0 255 36511 X

,12.50

Misguided Virtue

False Notions of Corporate Social Responsibility

David Henderson

Hobart Paper 142; ISBN 0 255 36510 1

£12.50

HIV and Aids in Schools

The Political Economy of Pressure Groups and Miseducation

Barrie Craven, Pauline Dixon, Gordon Stewart & James Tooley

Occasional Paper 121; ISBN 0 255 36522 5

£10.00

The Road to Serfdom

The Reader's Digest *condensed version*

Friedrich A. Hayek

Occasional Paper 122; ISBN 0 255 36530 6

£7.50

Bastiat's *The Law*

Introduction by Norman Barry

Occasional Paper 123; ISBN 0 255 36509 8

£7.50

A Globalist Manifesto for Public Policy

Charles Calomiris

Occasional Paper 124; ISBN 0 255 36525 x

£7.50

Euthanasia for Death Duties

Putting Inheritance Tax Out of Its Misery

Barry Bracewell-Milnes

Research Monograph 54; ISBN 0 255 36513 6

£10.00

Liberating the Land

The Case for Private Land-use Planning

Mark Pennington

Hobart Paper 143; ISBN 0 255 36508 x

£10.00

IEA Yearbook of Government Performance 2002/2003

Edited by Peter Warburton

Yearbook 1; ISBN 0 255 36532 2

£15.00

Britain's Relative Economic Performance, 1870–1999

Nicholas Crafts

Research Monograph 55; ISBN 0 255 36524 1

£10.00

Should We Have Faith in Central Banks?

Otmar Issing

Occasional Paper 125; ISBN 0 255 36528 4

£7.50

The Dilemma of Democracy

Arthur Seldon

Hobart Paper 136 (reissue); ISBN 0 255 36536 5

£10.00

Capital Controls: a 'Cure' Worse Than the Problem?

Forrest Capie

Research Monograph 56; ISBN 0 255 36506 3

£10.00

The Poverty of 'Development Economics'
Deepak Lal
Hobart Paper 144 (reissue); ISBN 0 255 36519 5
£15.00

Should Britain Join the Euro?
The Chancellor's Five Tests Examined
Patrick Minford
Occasional Paper 126; ISBN 0 255 36527 6
£7.50

Post-Communist Transition: Some Lessons
Leszek Balcerowicz
Occasional Paper 127; ISBN 0 255 36533 0
£7.50

A Tribute to Peter Bauer
John Blundell et al.
Occasional Paper 128; ISBN 0 255 36531 4
£10.00

Employment Tribunals
Their Growth and the Case for Radical Reform
J. R. Shackleton
Hobart Paper 145; ISBN 0 255 36515 2
£10.00

Fifty Economic Fallacies Exposed

Geoffrey E. Wood

Occasional Paper 129; ISBN 0 255 36518 7

£12.50

A Market in Airport Slots

Keith Boyfield (editor), David Starkie, Tom Bass & Barry Humphreys

Readings 56; ISBN 0 255 36505 5

£10.00

Money, Inflation and the Constitutional Position of the Central Bank

Milton Friedman & Charles A. E. Goodhart

Readings 57; ISBN 0 255 36538 1

£10.00

railway.com

Parallels between the Early British Railways and the ICT Revolution

Robert C. B. Miller

Research Monograph 57; ISBN 0 255 36534 9

£12.50

The Regulation of Financial Markets

Edited by Philip Booth & David Currie

Readings 58; ISBN 0 255 36551 9

£12.50

Climate Alarmism Reconsidered
Robert L. Bradley Jr
Hobart Paper 146; ISBN 0 255 36541 1
£12.50

Government Failure: E. G. West on Education
Edited by James Tooley & James Stanfield
Occasional Paper 130; ISBN 0 255 36552 7
£12.50

Waging the War of Ideas
John Blundell
Second edition
Occasional Paper 131; ISBN 0 255 36547 0
£12.50

Corporate Governance: Accountability in the Marketplace
Elaine Sternberg
Second edition
Hobart Paper 147; ISBN 0 255 36542 X
£12.50

The Land Use Planning System

Evaluating Options for Reform

John Corkindale

Hobart Paper 148; ISBN 0 255 36550 0

£10.00

Economy and Virtue

Essays on the Theme of Markets and Morality

Edited by Dennis O'Keeffe

Readings 59; ISBN 0 255 36504 7

£12.50

Free Markets Under Siege

Cartels, Politics and Social Welfare

Richard A. Epstein

Occasional Paper 132; ISBN 0 255 36553 5

£10.00

Unshackling Accountants

D. R. Myddelton

Hobart Paper 149; ISBN 0 255 36559 4

£12.50

The Euro as Politics

Pedro Schwartz

Research Monograph 58; ISBN 0 255 36535 7

£12.50

Pricing Our Roads

Vision and Reality

Stephen Glaister & Daniel J. Graham

Research Monograph 59; ISBN 0 255 36562 4

£10.00

The Role of Business in the Modern World

Progress, Pressures, and Prospects for the Market Economy

David Henderson

Hobart Paper 150; ISBN 0 255 36548 9

£12.50

Public Service Broadcasting Without the BBC?

Alan Peacock

Occasional Paper 133; ISBN 0 255 36565 9

£10.00

The ECB and the Euro: the First Five Years

Otmar Issing

Occasional Paper 134; ISBN 0 255 36555 1

£10.00

Towards a Liberal Utopia?

Edited by Philip Booth

Hobart Paperback 32; ISBN 0 255 36563 2

£15.00

The Way Out of the Pensions Quagmire

Philip Booth & Deborah Cooper

Research Monograph 60; ISBN 0 255 36517 9

£12.50

Black Wednesday

A Re-examination of Britain's Experience in the Exchange Rate Mechanism

Alan Budd

Occasional Paper 135; ISBN 0 255 36566 7

£7.50

Crime: Economic Incentives and Social Networks

Paul Ormerod

Hobart Paper 151; ISBN 0 255 36554 3

£10.00

The Road to Serfdom *with* The Intellectuals and Socialism

Friedrich A. Hayek

Occasional Paper 136; ISBN 0 255 36576 4

£10.00

Money and Asset Prices in Boom and Bust

Tim Congdon

Hobart Paper 152; ISBN 0 255 36570 5

£10.00

To order copies of currently available IEA papers, or to enquire about availability, please contact:

Lavis Marketing
IEA orders
FREEPOST LON21280
Oxford OX3 7BR

Tel: 01865 767575
Fax: 01865 750079
Email: orders@lavismarketing.co.uk

The IEA also offers a subscription service to its publications. For a single annual payment, currently £40.00 in the UK, you will receive every monograph the IEA publishes during the course of a year and discounts on our extensive back catalogue. For more information, please contact:

Adam Myers
Subscriptions
The Institute of Economic Affairs
2 Lord North Street
London SW1P 3LB

Tel: 020 7799 8920
Fax: 020 7799 2137
Website: www.iea.org.uk